Government by Proxy

Government by Proxy
(Mis?)Managing Federal Programs

Donald F. Kettl
University of Virginia

A Division of Congressional Quarterly Inc.
1414 22nd Street N.W., Washington, D.C. 20037

Printed in the United States of America

Library of Congress Cataloging-in-Publication Data

Kettl, Donald F.
    Government by proxy.

    Includes index.
    1. Public contracts—United States. 2. Grants-in-aid—United States. 3. Tax expenditures—United States. 4. Government lending—United States. 5. Trade regulation—United States. I. Title.
HD3861.U6K47   1988   353.009   87-13645
ISBN 0-87187-429-6

For Mildred and Al

Contents

Contents

Preface

Cynicism about the performance of government programs is far too common these days. Lively newspaper stories report that the Pentagon buys hammers at ridiculously high prices, that wealthy citizens evade income taxes, and that student loans pay for home remodeling. Congressional committees investigate the performance of federal grant programs and the effectiveness of air safety regulations.

This book is dedicated to a simple proposition: government programs can indeed be managed well, but doing so is becoming more complicated. Some of the problems are the product of greed and abuse, but many more are the result of failures of managers—in government and in the private sector—to adapt to new and expanding forms of government action. Governments at all levels are relying increasingly on proxies—third parties such as corporations and private citizens—to produce the services for which the government pays. This administrative approach is complex, and it encompasses a wide range of programs: contracts, grants, tax expenditures, loans, and regulation.

Together these strategies—which I call "government by proxy"—represent the vast bulk of federal government activities and a growing share of state and local activities as well. Moreover, they pose an important administrative challenge because the U.S. government only indirectly controls the proxies that produce its goods and services. Each policy strategy has its own unique problems, and successfully managing each one requires matching special skills to the needs of the strategy. This challenge, not surprisingly, often presents tremendous problems—such as those described in the chapters that follow. However, as the conclusion of each chapter demonstrates, failure is not inevitable. Success can come through the skillful application of managerial techniques that address each strategy's specific needs.

I am greatly indebted to several organizations for their support of this book. Both the University of Virginia and the Thomas Jefferson Memorial Foundation generously funded a leave from teaching during which I completed the book. In addition, the National Institute for Dispute Resolution provided a grant for the research and development of the "success" stories that conclude Chapters 2 through 6. Robert Jones of NIDR was especially helpful to me in locating pertinent studies for Chapters 3, 5, and 6. Chris Kirtz of the U.S. Environmental Protection Agency shared his experience in negotiated rule making, which enriched Chapter 6.

Several colleagues read the manuscript in its entirety and made comments that greatly improved its content. I am grateful to Laurence J. O'Toole of Auburn University, James S. Bowman of Florida State University, and Frederick C. Mosher of the University of Virginia for their care in reviewing the book.

In addition, I wish to give my deep thanks to Joanne Daniels and her staff at CQ Press, who enthusiastically backed the project from its inception. In particular, I am enormously indebted to Carolyn McGovern, who worked tirelessly to sharpen the book's style, and to Tracy White, who carefully oversaw its production.

Finally, my wife, Sue, has patiently tolerated a sometimes difficult writer through each draft of the book. No author could wish for more support, and she has my lasting love.

Donald F. Kettl
Charlottesville, Virginia

The paradox of limited government

1

Tales of abuse of government programs make great newspaper stories. In 1985 readers learned about Defense Department purchases of $435 hammers and $659 ashtrays, and also about an inflation rate for the Pentagon of 2,500 percent over sixteen months in landing gear clamps.

Following on the heels of these stories came charges that coffee-brewing machines for the Air Force's C-5A jet transport cost $7,400, more than double the amount Delta Airlines and TWA paid for similar machines—and more than twice what the Air Force itself paid for similar coffee machines in the transport's sister airplane, the C-5B.

Some Air Force officials defended the coffee machine. It was, they said, "actually a Hot Beverage Unit," and the price was "fair and reasonable" for a piece of equipment on a military transport. An Air Force general, however, admitted that the price was "ludicrous." The enormous cost, it turned out, could be traced to custom requirements of the Air Force that made the machine nearly indestructible. The machine was designed to produce fifty-six ounces of coffee, tea, or hot soup every four minutes, even if the plane were to lose all cabin pressure or were to be subjected to 40g's, enough gravitational force to kill everyone on board. This specially designed machine resulted from a procurement system that custom-engineered many products, a system that bought "hot beverage units" instead of off-the-shelf coffee makers and "hexagonal alignment tools" instead of hardware-store allen wrenches.[1]

While these stories make entertaining reading, they have fed a pervasive cynicism about government performance. Such incidents have

1

capped a decade of growing suspicion that government programs were inherently wasteful and inefficient and that most just did not work well. A public opinion survey found that 78 percent of Americans in 1980 thought that people in government wasted a lot of tax money. In 1958 the number was only 43 percent. A 1981 Gallup poll, in fact, revealed that those responding thought the federal government wasted 48 cents of every dollar. State and local governments were considered more efficient, but they were scarcely on the citizens' honor roll. Respondents believed that state governments wasted 29 cents of each tax dollar, and local governments 23 cents.[2]

This sentiment had begun to surface years before. In 1969 management expert Peter F. Drucker complained, "There is mounting evidence that government is big rather than strong; that it is fat and flabby rather than powerful; that it costs a great deal but does not achieve much." Drucker argued that "government is sick," competent only in waging war and creating inflation. He sadly concluded, "Modern government has become ungovernable."[3]

Among scholars, dissatisfaction with government performance produced a new school of analysis called *implementation,* the study of the administration of governmental policy. When they looked at program implementation, scholars came to distressingly similar conclusions. Randall B. Ripley and Grace A. Franklin wrote, "Domestic programs virtually never achieve all that is expected of them."[4] Eugene Bardach concluded, "It is excruciatingly hard to implement [programs] in a way that pleases anyone at all."[5] Scholarly study thus reaffirmed the message in the news: government programs are not run well, and they achieve poor results. Americans harbor deep concerns about the ability of their government to perform. "It appears that the trend of declining trust in government is focused on the performance of government and the behavior of public officials, and not on the system itself or the institutions and norms associated with it," reported public opinion experts Seymour Martin Lipset and William Schneider.[6]

What produced this general loss of faith? The public's perceptions of federal programs gone awry result not so much from poor government performance as from great expectations. Especially in the ambitious years of the Great Society during the 1960s, we dreamed such big dreams—to train the unemployed for jobs, to provide housing for the homeless, and most of all to end poverty—that disappointment was inevitable. In reaching perhaps too far, our grasp fell short.

In part, the problem has been the size of government itself. Large organizations can take advantage of many economies of scale, but they are usually harder to run. Coordination and communication are more

2

Figure 1-1 Federal payroll and government spending, 1950-1984 (in millions of constant 1982 dollars)

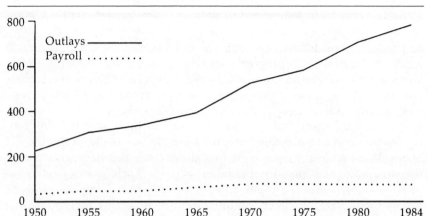

Sources: U.S. Bureau of the Census, *Statistical Abstract of the United States* (Washington, D.C.: U.S. Government Printing Office, various years); and U.S. Office of Management and Budget, *Budget of the United States Government, Historical Tables, Fiscal Year 1987* (Washington, D.C.: U.S. Government Printing Office, 1986).

Note: "Payroll" is annual expenditures on civilian salaries.

complex. It is difficult to get good information up to managers so they can have an accurate view of what is happening on the front lines.

There is truth in each of these explanations, but none of them completely explain the problems we observe around us. A far more powerful argument is that government programs themselves have changed. While the programs have grown enormously in size—more than two and three-fourths times, even allowing for inflation, from 1955 to 1985—the federal bureaucracy has not. The number of civilians working for the federal government grew only 25 percent over the same period—and from 1967 to 1985 there was virtually no increase. As Figure 1-1 shows, in fact, the federal civilian payroll has stayed about the same, allowing for inflation, while federal spending has grown.

Defining government by proxy

What accounts for this paradox of larger federal programs without a larger federal bureaucracy? The answer lies in the growth of *government by proxy.* Especially since World War II, the federal government has developed a vast network of new policy strategies to administer its programs. Contracting has grown enormously, and there has been an explosive growth in federal aid to state and local governments. A maze of new regulations governs not only the availability but also the safety of products. The federal government has become the nation's largest lender through its loan programs, and the growth of tax preferences has taken an ever-larger bite out of tax collections. In addition, the federal government has created quasi-governmental corporations, such as Amtrak and the postal service, to deliver public services.

To be sure, there is nothing new in any of these schemes. Military contracting and the postal service, for example, are as old as the United States. What *is* new, however, is that these strategies have grown into the predominant form of government activity. Each strategy relies on proxies—intermediaries responsible for actually producing the goods or services—in place of direct administration of programs by the government.

In government contracts, these goods or services are only as good as the contractor's performance. The success of federal grant programs hinges on the actions of the state and local governments carrying out the programs. The effects of regulations depend on how well industries and individuals comply with the rules. Loan programs and tax preferences are designed to influence the incentives of producers and consumers, and their result depends on how those incentives work. Thus, many more government programs depend for their effectiveness not only on the government's performance but also on how hundreds of millions of Americans behave as the government's proxies. In fact, every time an American fills out an income tax form, he or she is a partner in executing a remarkable range of government policies, such as incentives encouraging home ownership or contributions to charities. As Table 1-1 illustrates, government-by-proxy programs account for a substantial share of federal spending: 32 percent of the federal budget in fiscal year 1985 (that is, the federal government's budget year ending in 1985). If we add to this the government's expenditures for financing the national debt and transfers to individuals (for instance, social security payments), we discover that the federal government spends only about 14 percent of its budget on programs it administers itself—and about half of this amount goes to operations, maintenance, and personnel in the armed forces.[7] Furthermore, the federal government engages in programs of staggering size—especially tax breaks, loans, and regulation—whose costs are not reflected in the budget.

Government by proxy is an important but little-studied feature of governmental action. A few pioneering scholars—especially Frederick

4

Table 1-1 Federal expenditures, fiscal year 1985 budget

	Amount in billions of dollars	*Percent of total*
Interest on debt	129.4	14
Direct services		
Transfers	377.5	40
All other [a]	133.9	14
Indirect services		
Contracts	199.8	21
Grants	105.7	11
Total outlays	946.3	100

Sources: U.S. Office of Management and Budget, *Budget of the United States Government, Fiscal Year 1987: Historical Tables* (Washington, D.C.: U.S. Government Printing Office, 1986); and U.S. General Services Administration, *Federal Procurement Data System Standard Report, Fiscal Year 1985 Fourth Quarter* (Washington, D.C.: U.S. Government Printing Office, 1986).

[a] Estimated from other amounts.

C. Mosher, Lester M. Salamon, and Harold Seidman—have identified the issue as a crucial one.[8] The phenomenon goes by many names, from Salamon's "third-party government" to "indirect administration" to "government by proxy," as Seidman and Robert Gilmour put it.[9] These writers have opened the door to our understanding one of the most complicated, difficult, and interesting phenomena of modern American government.

In the pages that follow, I will use the term *government by proxy* to describe the crucial relationships between the federal government and the third parties that ultimately administer the programs.

Forms of government by proxy

A quick survey of the various forms of government by proxy charts just how sweeping its role is in federal activities.

   1. *Contracts.* The federal government contracts with the private sector for many of its goods and services. The Defense Department is the government's largest buyer, but contracting is an

5

important strategy throughout the rest of the government, from the management of concession stands in the national parks to the writing of research studies. Contracts accounted for 21 percent of all federal spending in 1985.

2. *Grants to state and local governments.* For a century the federal government has provided substantial grants to state and local governments, so they will do what the federal government wants done. State governments build interstate highways and manage welfare. Local governments construct public housing and provide mass transit. Together, grants to state and local governments totaled 11 percent of 1985 federal spending.

In addition to these programs, the federal government has developed extensive programs whose full cost the budget does not capture.

3. *Tax expenditures.* Over the years, the federal government has created a complex set of incentives through the tax code. Some people know them as "tax preferences," some as "tax breaks," and some simply as "loopholes" ("tax breaks" are *my* valuable incentives—"loopholes" are always *someone else's* abuse of the tax system). Tax deductions for interest on home mortgages and for charitable contributions are perhaps the most well known and most popular, but the array of tax preferences is truly staggering. Before the revolutionary tax reform bill of 1986, they amounted to more than 40 percent of all federal revenues and were three-fourths as large as revenue from the federal personal income tax.[10] Even after tax reform, though, they still represented a substantial use of resources to influence the behavior of taxpayers. By inducing people to do things they might not otherwise have done, tax expenditures have become an important policy strategy.

4. *Loan programs.* The federal government is the country's biggest banker: by 1985, the federal government was actively making or assisting more than $1 trillion in loans.[11] Through these loans, the federal government makes capital available for everything from student loans to home mortgages. The government's goal is to make credit cheaper than it would cost in the private market or to make credit available when the private sector might not provide it at all.

5. *Regulation.* Finally, the federal government has put together a vast network of rules governing the activity of every business and every person in the country. Federal rules determine the cost and availability of many private-sector goods and services. They

govern the safety of consumer goods such as toys and drugs. While the cost of regulations is unknown and largely unmeasurable, it is unquestionably large.

Government by proxy is not just a federal strategy; it is an approach to governance that state and local governments are adopting as well. Smaller cities, for example, frequently contract out services like legal counsel and equipment maintenance. Throughout the country, refuse collection is frequently contracted out, as are over 50 percent of the social services funded by Title XX grants to state governments.[12] The issues of government by proxy thus apply across the board to modern government in the United States.

The growth of government by proxy

What has caused the growth of government by proxy? The factors responsible are varied and complex, but they turn on four developments: the scope of the government's mission, the technological challenges of modern society, the budget constraints of the post-Vietnam era, and the impact of theoretical arguments supporting the use of proxies.

The government's mission

The government is no longer responsible just for delivering the mail, conducting foreign relations, and protecting the national defense. After the Great Depression, the federal government took on basic responsibility for steering the economy and putting its citizens to work. Since World War II, furthermore, the federal government has built a substantial defense establishment and has further broadened its social programs, from rebuilding cities to ensuring minimum income for the poor and the elderly. "In many ways," economist Murray Weidenbaum writes, "government today is charged with ultimate responsibility for the employment and the basic welfare of the citizenry."[13]

The government's role has expanded dramatically. As a share of all goods and services produced in the economy (known as the gross national product), federal spending has grown from 10.8 percent in 1934 to 23.0 percent in 1987. Spending by all levels of government—federal, state, and local—was more than 40 percent of the gross national product in 1987.[14] Such a large role, quite simply, is too big for any organization to handle on its own. The growing use of proxies thus has been a natural reaction to the growth of government programs.

The technological challenge

Government programs not only have grown tremendously, but they have become far more complex as well. The development of atomic energy and manned space flight in the first two decades after World War II required unparalleled intellectual energy. Ever more sophisticated military weapons, from nuclear-tipped missiles to space-based defense systems, kept the national defense at the cutting edge of scientific research. Because no organization—not even the federal government— could collect the know-how needed to respond to all these technological challenges, the government increased its reliance on proxies, even for such regular activities as writing annual reports.

Budget constraints

The economic roller coaster that the Vietnam War started in the late 1960s doomed the federal budget to decades of deficits. Meanwhile, the taxpayer revolt of the late 1970s put sharp limits on the taxing ability of state and local governments.[15] The rising cost of government services coupled with limits on resources made new policy initiatives, such as the Great Society programs of the 1960s, impossible. Instead, governments tried imaginative new ways to get around spending limits and deficit politics. Most popular were quasi-market programs that promised greater efficiency and other programs—for instance, loans—whose full cost did not show up on the budget.

In the energy crisis of the late 1970s, when the deficit limited the Carter administration's ability to spend money to help people insulate their homes, Congress passed a new tax credit. Up to a certain limit, the money that taxpayers spent for insulation could be subtracted from their income tax bills. The federal government thus effectively paid for the insulation, but the cost did not show up on the budget. Likewise, when the budget deficit limited the growth of federal grants for higher education, the federal government made it easier to qualify for guaranteed student loans. The cost of the guarantees appeared nowhere on the budget, and the federal government was liable only for the cost of defaults, which were unpredictable and which, in any event, lay in the future. Such off-budget programs proved attractive when the budget was tight.

Theoretical arguments

Much of the growth of government by proxy, thus, was a pragmatic response to new problems. However, the increasing use of proxies also

8

had substantial intellectual support, in part from old theories of decentralization and self-government and in part from much newer theories of public choice.

Decentralization and self-government. The modern American state is, in some ways, paradoxical. Americans have always had a fiercely romantic belief in limited government, a government whose power would never be so great as to endanger their freedom. Yet Americans have thrust increasingly more ambitious goals on their government, from the exploration of space to the welfare of citizens. The American response to both limited government and self-government has been decentralization: to rely on state and local governments, as well as private-sector organizations and ordinary citizens, to carry out many of the tasks government undertakes.

Decentralization can take two forms.[16] In *administrative decentralization* the government delegates the responsibility for managing programs, as well as the authority needed to do so. At the same time, the government retains the power to study the results, order changes, and even to revoke the authority if performance does not measure up. By signing a contract with a private company to supply food and beverage services in a national park, for example, the federal government allows the contractor to decide (within the terms of the contract) what to sell and how. If the contractor's performance is unsatisfactory, the government can recommend changes, refuse to renew the contract, or in egregious cases revoke the contract before its term expires.

In *political decentralization,* on the other hand, the basic decision-making power itself is given to independent decision makers, who alone are responsible for how they use it. The American system of federalism, for example, vests the states with powers not otherwise given to the federal government, and they are free to exercise them as they wish— provided they do not trample on rights guaranteed by the U.S. Constitution.

While government by proxy relies on both approaches to decentralization, it is at its core a hybrid approach. Government by proxy is distinctive, Salamon contends, because it means the *sharing* of a "basic governmental function: the exercise of discretion over the use of public authority and the spending of public funds." [17] Government by proxy is both more than administrative decentralization (the sharing of authority is typically very broad) and less than political decentralization (the government does not leave authority solely with the proxies).

Thus, the American tradition of self-government provides an important intellectual base for the growth of government by proxy. It does not, however, give firm advice on how to handle the difficult challenge of managing such a hybrid.

Public choice. A more recent intellectual contribution, an economic theory known as "public choice," supplies further support for the growth of government by proxy.[18] So influential are the proponents of this school, in fact, that one of its leading spokesmen, James M. Buchanan, won the 1986 Nobel Prize in economics. Public choice theory, furthermore, provided the basis for much of the Reagan administration's efforts to pare back government and to turn more functions over to the private sector, a movement known as "privatization."

Public choice theory seeks to explain how the government makes choices. It begins, as do many economic theories, with the simple assumption that human beings are rational and seek to maximize the things that are important to them. Rationality and self-interest may lead government employees to work toward enhancing their job security and increasing their agency's budget. A collection of bureaucrats each pursuing his or her own self-interest, as Gordon Tullock argued in *The Politics of Bureaucracy,* is likely to produce results that are both inefficient and not in the public interest.[19] The larger the bureaucracy, furthermore, the greater the problem of pursuit of personal interest is likely to be.

President Ronald Reagan in 1982 appointed a commission headed by industrialist J. Peter Grace to identify opportunities to increase efficiency and reduce costs in the federal government. In its report the Grace Commission relied on public choice theory to point out what it saw as the three key problems in government programs administered by government bureaucrats. First, the commission argued that higher appropriations and more staff are an agency's rewards for inefficient management. Agencies and their officials have no incentives to return money to the Treasury, while spending all of the budget is the easiest way to make the case for more money. Second, government is insulated from competition and, therefore, need not respond to changes as, the report alleged, businesses in the private sector must if they are to succeed. (However, competition is no guarantee of adaptation, as the failure of American steel and automobile manufacturing to modernize will attest.) Third, powerful constituencies grow up around government programs. These constituencies, representing groups such as bankers, manufacturers, labor unions, and the elderly, become comfortable with the status quo and fight government attempts to force them to change and adapt.[20]

The public choice movement's answer to these problems is to "privatize," to rely more on the private sector for achieving the government's goals. "Privatization," as the Grace Commission put it, means "to *provide* services without *producing* them." [21] Privatization can take two basic routes: the transfer of as many programs as possible to the private sector (where, proponents believe, the pressures of competition will improve efficiency); and, for those programs that remain governmental, more reliance on the private sector (with its allegedly superior incentives) to administer them. Government would make the basic decisions, but the private sector, to the extent possible, would implement them.

Public choice theory, with the accompanying argument for privatization, became a powerful engine driving the growth of government by proxy during the 1960s, but it has taken on new force since the beginning of the Reagan administration. One advocate, Stuart Butler, sees privatization as a kind of "political guerrilla warfare" that directs demand away from government growth.[22] Its proponents believe therefore that privatization provides a solid opportunity to reduce the size of government and balance the federal budget.

Fundamental questions of public choice

The public choice argument, however, raises three fundamental issues of central concern to government by proxy. First, what should be privatized? There are some programs that should not be handed over to the private sector—but which ones? Second, are the assumptions of public choice valid? The very simplicity of the argument gives it much power, but its simple assumptions about the behavior of government bureaucrats raise troublesome questions. Finally, even if its arguments are valid, privatization substitutes a new set of administrative problems for the old ones. Contracts, as the newspaper stories about mismanagement of Pentagon purchasing make very clear, do not administer themselves.

What should be "privatized"?

Arguments for privatization bring together two related but very different issues: what government should do and how it should do it. The public choice school argues that because government cannot run very large operations effectively it should not try to do too much. The privatization debate, however, is often more complicated because it muddles the questions of ends (what government should do) and means (how government should do it).

11

The debate is sometimes a difficult semantic one. Butler calls "load shedding," the transfer of responsibility to the private sector for what had been public-sector programs, "the only mechanism that could be called privatization." [23] Indeed, this argument spins off Drucker's statement that the best route to solving "the sickness of government" is to "reprivatize," to return to the private sector those functions that government has taken over from it. [24]

James L. Sundquist protests that such abandonment of federal responsibility to private enterprise is "false" privatization. [25] If we agree with the argument for privatization, it is because we believe the private sector is more efficient, that it does not devote resources to activities that do not produce income. The government has taken on many functions, however, precisely because the private sector either will not do them or would not do them in a way that respects competing values such as equality, for instance, over efficiency. "True" privatization, Sundquist argues, means shifting the performance, and not the responsibility, for the work.

This debate is crucial because it hinges on a central question: which functions are, at their core, *public,* those for which the public sector has basic responsibility? That is a broad issue indeed—one that speaks to one's individual values. Without trying to answer that question here, we can say that there are some things—national defense, for instance—that we would not wish to delegate to the private sector. Neither would we want to delegate matters involving questions of basic rights, such as preventing discrimination in employment or destruction of the environment. In fact, the pursuit of public policy often means making difficult tradeoffs between competing values, such as equality and efficiency. [26] Deciding what to delegate to proxies and under what conditions thus is a crucial question that privatization does not answer.

The public interest or self-interest?

Much of the force of the public choice argument comes from its logical clarity and simplicity. It is at once a capsule diagnosis of government's ills and a compact prescription for how to cure them. The power of this logic, however, rests on its basic assumption of the bureaucrat as a rational being: that the administrator single-mindedly concentrates on what is of ultimate utility to himself or herself, and that this perspective revolves around personal power, security, and income.

It is hard to argue that individuals do not look to enhance their own positions. However, it is equally difficult to accept the notion that in administering government programs bureaucrats drive so hard to maximize their own utility that other, more publicly oriented objectives slip out of sight. The number of public-spirited bureaucrats is in reality quite large, and an approach to public policy that starts with such a cynical view of public servants is dangerously flawed. The search for an easy, parsimonious explanation can get in the way of understanding the complexities of managing government programs.

At the same time, though, public choice theory makes an important contribution. It emphasizes that different participants in any given program have different values and motives and that these values and motives influence the roles that individuals play in the political process. This is an especially important element in government by proxy, which relies so heavily on state and local government officials, as well as on private-sector employees and individual citizens. Each participant has his or her own motives. These differences in motives, therefore, pose a significant problem for effective management.

How should privatization be administered?

Public choice advocates typically assume that the self-regulating features of the market will solve any problems plaguing publicly administered programs. The long history of government grants and contracts, as well as the more recent newspaper tales of waste, fraud, and abuse, offer ample proof that this is not so. The American Federation of State, County, and Municipal Employees, for example, compiled a lengthy collection of stories illustrating that privatization-as-contracting often breeds its own problems, from poor performance to bribery and fraud.[27]

The point is very simple yet often overlooked, especially by proponents of the public choice school: government-by-proxy programs do not administer themselves. Rather, they generate their own set of administrative problems that must be solved if they are to be successful. If directly administered programs are managed by self-interested bureaucrats, government-by-proxy programs are managed by self-interested proxies, each seeking to maximize its *own* utility, sometimes at the government's expense. Different groups will inevitably have different values; but when programs involve both public and private organizations, the differences are magnified. Each program must be carefully administered to ensure high accountability and performance.

There thus is an irreducible governmental role in shaping government by proxy. Indeed, the spread of government by proxy means that the public-private distinction is no longer very distinct. Where can the line be drawn in a defense contract in which a private contractor builds products it can sell only to the Pentagon, according to Pentagon specifications, and under the supervision of Pentagon inspectors? Or in the private housing market, supported by the federal government through extensive tax breaks and loan programs? As Brian O'Connell, president of Independent Sector, a Washington-based group representing nonprofit organizations, put it, government programs are moving increasingly to "abject interdependence." [28]

In managing that interdependence, three lessons are clear. First, government by proxy is different from directly administered programs and thus requires different kinds of management from other programs. Second, different government-by-proxy programs require subtly different administrative techniques. As Salamon writes, each strategy has its own "political economy." [29] Third, government by proxy inevitably produces deep conflicts in values, and those conflicts predictably cause serious problems in performance and accountability.

In many ways, government by proxy is nothing new. The Army has been buying goods by contract for two hundred years, and federal grants to state governments date from the early years of the Republic. However, especially since World War II, we have seen an important trend: the increasing reliance on government by proxy by governments at all levels. The actual size of government by proxy is confoundingly difficult to measure, but it is probably no exaggeration to argue that it now constitutes the majority of the federal government's operations, as well as an important part of state and local activity.

Interdependence and the public interest _____

It would be easy to argue that the growth of government by proxy, and especially the government's difficulties in controlling its proxies, has caused the poor performance of federal programs. Could it be that overpriced coffee makers are the inevitable product of greedy government contractors? Are wealthy, profitable corporations that pay no income tax simply the inevitable result of a tax system out of control?

This argument is far too simple, however. Government by proxy is neither necessarily better nor worse than direct government management of public services. Rather, it is fundamentally *different*. More and more, the performance of government programs depends on the interdependence between government and its proxies. Distinctions among the federal, state, and local governments and between the public and private sectors are rapidly losing their original meaning. As Don K. Price recognized in 1965, the line between the two is more and more a false one. Public and private spheres, he explained, are becoming indistinguishable.[30] The conduct of government is increasingly a partnership among all members of society, in patterns that are often extremely complicated.

Implications of interdependence

This growing interdependence leads to several important propositions and problems.

1. *Sharing of authority.* As government relies more on proxies, it shares a significant amount of authority for its programs. Government by proxy means that important decisions about both what to do and how to do it are made, at least in part, by nongovernmental officials. If such interdependence is unavoidable, however, how should the government's authority be shared? Who ultimately is accountable to the public for performance?

2. *Differences in values.* Interdependence also means that, as people and organizations come to government by proxy, they bring different values and goals. The cultures of government and corporations, for example, vary widely. Government puts priority on consensus and compromise, the corporate world on profit and control. When these cultures collide, as inevitably they must in such programs, how can their values be reconciled?

3. *Management techniques.* Government by proxy has its own political economy: its political and economic issues differ from other forms of government action, and each government-by-proxy strategy raises different questions. This means that government managers must use different techniques in managing these strategies than they would use with direct government programs. They must also have a repertoire of techniques tailored to the special management needs of each strategy. Public administration, as economist Charles Schultze put it, "now encompasses the far more vexing question of how to change some aspects of the behavior of a whole society." [31] Which approaches work best on which problems?

These questions of authority, values, and management are extremely difficult to resolve. On the constitutional level, government cannot delegate away basic responsibility for its programs. On the political level, it carefully supervises those who exercise authority on its behalf. And on the administrative level, the government must delicately but imaginatively deal with these challenges to ensure the best possible performance.

Mixing systems

We can approach these puzzles by thinking about government by proxy as a realm where different participants—federal, state, and local, as well as public and private—interact.

In managing government by proxy, the government faces two central problems. First is the problem of synchronization of *goals*. For government-by-proxy programs to be effective, the government must try to get the proxy to behave as the government desires. Such programs are public programs, enacted with public goals in mind, and the foremost responsibility of administrators is to make sure that these public goals are served. Ensuring the primacy of public goals is thus the foremost problem of government by proxy. At the same time, of course, each proxy seeks its own goals. For government programs to work, these different goals must somehow mesh.

Second is the problem of *feedback*. Government needs to know what proxies are accomplishing with the programs—what goods or services they are producing, who is receiving loans for which purposes, and how state and local governments are spending grants. Obtaining reliable information is always a problem. Within bureaucracies, subordinates must condense information to a manageable size before passing it up to superiors. In addition, subordinates tend to pass on good news while suppressing bad news. Even at its best, therefore, feedback can become filtered and distorted.[32] When the information must come from outside the bureaucracy—from the proxy—the distortions and filtering can be even worse, because the manager cannot rely on regular bureaucratic channels. Good feedback, though, is essential not only for detecting noncompliance with the government's goals but also for helping the government adjust its goals as programs evolve.

Issuing orders might appear to be the best way to solve these problems. Authority and rulings, however, do not produce sure results even within bureaucracies. When a public program relies on the coordinated behavior of different organizations, both public and private, the management problem is magnified. Because each side needs the other, the relationship is in many ways reciprocal and cooperative; yet because each participant is directed by different domains, cultures, and goals, the government and the proxy are inherently in conflict. Government by proxy means balancing the natural interconnections and conflicts in working toward a program's goal.

Government by proxy is thus fundamentally a process of bringing different systems together to produce cooperatively some publicly defined end. Each system has its own features, functions, and missions that help shape an organization's ongoing behavior. The organizations must find what theorist James D. Thompson labels the "coalignment" of goals." [33] Systems theory suggests, furthermore, that the problem is an ongoing one. Every organization is constantly swirling and changing, carried along in a stream of actions. Successful federal managers must find a way to discover the "nexus," the intersection, of such streams in several different organizations and to position the program at this nexus. [34]

Systems theory also describes how organizations will behave in trying to find this nexus. [35] In the short run, organizations (both government and its proxies) seek certainty. No one likes to be surprised. Sudden budget cuts can cripple productivity and cost people their jobs. Managers react to unfavorable media coverage of their programs by worrying more about damage control than about correcting ongoing programs. Administrators naturally seek to avoid sudden changes and crises.

Yet the quest for stability and control can lead to rigidity, discouraging organizations and their managers from adapting to new problems and opportunities. The opportunities for change may take different forms, and new problems may force agencies to adapt. An incoming president may have ambitious plans for new programs; government agencies and their proxies alike naturally try to position themselves to take advantage of them. Likewise, new technology or population shifts prompt organizations to change as well. The March of Dimes is the classic case of the flexible organization. It set out to raise money to stop polio—a goal that was achieved when researchers found a vaccine that could prevent this dreaded disease. The organization then faced an important choice: to disband or to take on a new cause. Its managers chose the course of flexibility and announced that the March of Dimes henceforth would battle birth defects. Any organization will seek such flexibility in the long run and alter its mission if necessary to remain in business.

The great problem, of course, is that these aims are contradictory. An organization cannot simultaneously enjoy certainty and flexibility. This is, in Thompson's phrase, "the paradox of administration" that governs the interactions between government and its proxies. [36] Government quite naturally seeks certainty from its proxies: it wants guaranteed output in exchange for its money. The proxies, on the other hand, want the most flexibility possible in meeting the government's goals. No

17

contractor wants to get locked into a bargain that allows no maneuvering room if circumstances change. We can turn the tables and look at the problem in reverse. The proxies naturally want a predictable flow of money from the government, while the government wants flexibility in shaping its goals—in the specifications of new weapons systems, for instance. Government thus is likely to want flexibility when the proxies want certainty, and certainty when the proxies want flexibility. The conflicting approaches of government and its proxies are an obstacle to finding out where their goals intersect and what actually happens in government programs.

Approaches to government by proxy _____

It is far too easy to attribute our dissatisfaction with government policy to contractors' greed or mismanagement or to bureaucrats' self-interest. The real issues are far more subtle. They revolve around the fundamental transformation in government policy that government by proxy represents. They revolve as well around the basic conflicts of values inevitably created by policy strategies involving different, interdependent organizations.

Conflict, indeed, is unavoidable because, as with any relationship between large and complex systems, the government-proxy relationship is dynamic and difficult. Because we expect different organizations to have different objectives, problems are likely to be the norm, not the exception. Both sides in the relationship are likely to seek, simultaneously, incompatible goals. In addition, there is the final issue special to governmental programs. Government by proxy requires more than finding a common ground—a "coalignment"—among different organizations. All of these programs were established by Congress in concert with the president; their values have a higher legitimacy than those of private organizations. It is one thing to find a mutually acceptable accommodation between two different groups. It is often quite another—and much more difficult—to find that common ground while keeping the public interest foremost.

These key issues—goals and feedback—provide a guide through the chapters that follow. How does the government pursue its goals, and what problems does it encounter? How well does it discover what actually happens with its programs? Each chapter examines a different government-by-proxy strategy and begins with an example of what happens when the interaction between government and its proxies goes very wrong. Each chapter ends with an illustration of a more effective approach to resolving these problems.

The book thus is neither a complaint against modern American government nor a cynical look at the extreme abuses that government by proxy sometimes produces. Neither is it a criticism of the growing reach of government programs, which is a very different philosophical question. Quite simply, this book is an argument that the changing forms of government action require imaginative public administration, tailored carefully to the specific problems of government by proxy in its different forms.

Notes

1. *Washington Post*, September 20, 1984, A1; February 12, 1986, A17.
2. Seymour Martin Lipset and William Schneider, *The Confidence Gap* (New York: Free Press, 1983), 17, 304.
3. Peter F. Drucker, "The Sickness of Government," *The Public Interest*, no. 14 (Winter 1969): 3, 7, 8.
4. Randall B. Ripley and Grace A. Franklin, *Policy Implementation and Bureaucracy*, 2d ed. (Chicago: Dorsey Press, 1986), 2.
5. Eugene Bardach, *The Implementation Game* (Cambridge: MIT Press, 1977), 3.
6. Lipset and Schneider, *The Confidence Gap*, 29.
7. See the discussion in Frederick C. Mosher, "The Changing Responsibilities and Tactics of the Federal Government," *Public Administration Review* 40 (November/December 1980): 542.
8. Ibid.; Lester M. Salamon, "Rethinking Public Management: Third-Party Government and the Changing Forms of Government Action," *Public Policy* 29 (Summer 1981): 255–275; Salamon, "The Rise of Third-Party Government: Implications for Public Management," speech delivered to the National Academy of Public Administration, Spring Meeting, Washington, D.C., June 5, 1986; and Harold Seidman and Robert Gilmour, *Politics, Position, and Power*, 4th ed. (New York: Oxford University Press, 1986).
9. Salamon, "The Rise of Third-Party Government," 255; Seidman and Gilmour, *Politics, Position, and Power*, 128.
10. John F. Witte, *The Politics and Development of the Federal Income Tax* (Madison: University of Wisconsin Press, 1985), 292.
11. U.S. Office of Management and Budget, *Budget of the United States Government, Fiscal Year 1987, Special Analyses* (Washington, D.C.: U.S. Government Printing Office, 1986).
12. Jeffrey D. Straussman, "More Bang for Fewer Bucks? Or How Local Government Can Rediscover the Potentials (and Pitfalls) of the Market," *Public Administration Review* 41 (January 1981): 151.
13. Murray L. Weidenbaum, *The Modern Public Sector* (New York: Basic Books, 1969), 7.

14. U.S. Office of Management and Budget, *Budget of the United States Government, Fiscal Year 1988, Historical Tables* (Washington, D.C.: U.S. Government Printing Office, 1987), 1.2(1)-(2).
15. Straussman, "More Bang for Fewer Bucks?" 151.
16. See James W. Fesler, "Approaches to the Understanding of Decentralization," *Journal of Politics* 27 (August 1965): 536-566; and Weidenbaum, *The Modern Public Sector*, 198-199.
17. Salamon, "The Rise of Third-Party Government."
18. For a fuller discussion, see Donald F. Kettl, "Performance and Accountability: The Challenge to Public Administration" (Occasional paper prepared for the National Academy of Public Administration, Washington, D.C., 1987).
19. Gordon Tullock, *The Politics of Bureaucracy* (Washington, D.C.: Public Affairs Press, 1965); James M. Buchanan and Gordon Tullock, *The Calculus of Consent* (Ann Arbor: University of Michigan Press, 1962).
20. President's Private Sector Survey on Cost Control (Grace Commission), *Report on Privatization* (Washington, D.C.: U.S. Government Printing Office, 1983), vii.
21. Ibid., i.
22. Stuart M. Butler, *Privatizing Federal Spending* (New York: Universe Books, 1985), 58, 166.
23. Ibid., 52-57; see also E. S. Savas, *Privatizing the Public Sector* (Chatham, N.J.: Chatham House, 1982), 118-124.
24. Drucker, "The Sickness of Government," 17.
25. James L. Sundquist, "Privatization: No Panacea for What Ails Government," in *Public-Private Partnership*, ed. Harvey Brooks, Lance Leibman, and Corinne S. Schelling (Cambridge: Ballinger, 1984), 306-307.
26. See Arthur Okun, *Equality and Efficiency* (Washington, D.C.: Brookings, 1975).
27. American Federation of State, County, and Municipal Employees, *Passing the Bucks* (Washington, D.C.: AFSCME, 1984).
28. Quoted by Kettl, "Performance and Accountability"; compare Weidenbaum, *The Modern Public Sector*, 34.
29. Salamon, "Rethinking Public Management," 264.
30. Don K. Price, *The Scientific Estate* (Cambridge: Harvard University Press, 1965), 16.
31. Charles L. Schultze, *The Public Use of the Private Interest* (Washington, D.C.: Brookings, 1977), 12.
32. See Anthony Downs, *Inside Bureaucracy* (Boston: Little, Brown, 1967); Herbert Kaufman, *Administrative Feedback* (Washington, D.C.: Brookings, 1973).
33. James D. Thompson, *Organizations in Action* (New York: McGraw-Hill, 1967), 147.
34. Ibid. The term "nexus" is Thompson's.
35. Ibid., 150-152.
36. Ibid., 148.

Contracts: the gun that couldn't

2

Reporters jammed into the Pentagon press room one August day in 1985 to hear Defense Secretary Caspar W. Weinberger announce the cancellation of the contract for the Divad, the Division Air Defense gun. Designed to automate the job of locating and shooting down enemy aircraft before they could strike American tanks, the Divad was the Army's answer to advanced Soviet-bloc jets and helicopters. This self-propelled, tank-like weapon equipped with sophisticated radar, computer systems, and guns—had it worked—would have been fielded to protect Army tanks. Keeping American tanks rolling in the face of the Soviet bloc's overwhelming armored advantage was a keystone of the Army's contingency plans for a European ground war.

For Weinberger, the Divad decision was a two-edged sword. It fueled criticism that the Pentagon had lost control over the cost of weapons. Already beset by tales of $7,000 coffee makers, $90 screwdrivers, and $17.59 bolts, the Pentagon reeled under the $1.8 billion Divad loss. The same summer, in fact, brought reports that the Pentagon's own inspector general had found the Defense Department had misspent another $1.6 billion over several programs.[1] At the same time, though, Weinberger's decision deflected charges that the secretary had never met a weapon he didn't like. His staff suggested that Weinberger, when faced with clear evidence of serious problems, was willing to take strong action. With Weinberger's decision, the Defense Department shut down a weapon production line for the first time since the cancellation of the Army Cheyenne helicopter fifteen years earlier.

21

Divad production was to be a model of efficiency. To save time and money, Army planners decided to buy "off-the-shelf" components for the gun. The Army started with its M48 tank chassis to propel the weapon. Then it added twin forty-millimeter Swedish Bofors guns, radar from the Air Force's F16 fighter, and a laser range finder. By assembling the gun with already-tested parts, using an "accelerated acquisition strategy," Army officials hoped to save money and to halve the fourteen years typically required for developing of new weapons.

The new strategy proved to be disastrous, however. The tank chassis was seriously underpowered and did not have the speed to keep up with the M1 Abrams tanks it was designed to protect. Furthermore, the Bofors guns had a range of two-and-a-half miles, and new Soviet helicopters could potentially hover up to four miles away and knock out the tanks (and the Divads). Worse yet, the Divad's radar could not reliably locate and track attacking planes and helicopters. Divad "didn't work well enough," Weinberger conceded, to warrant spending $3 billion more to buy the 618 guns that the Army wanted.[2] Instead, he decided to stop the program and swallow the $1.8 billion already spent. The 65 Divads the Army already had bought would be relegated to experiments and would never see the field.

While the Army did keep costs under control, it never did get a working gun. The reason, as the U.S. General Accounting Office delicately put it, was that the gun was "less technically mature than anticipated." The Department of Defense's own testing office was more blunt. It reported that the gun was only slightly better than the Vulcan, the Army's existing gun; that it could not perform its mission; and that it proved difficult to maintain.[3] By pressing ahead with a system whose effectiveness was not proven, the Army spent nearly $2 billion on a gun it could not use.

Contracting as a policy tool

Contracting problems are nothing new. George Washington's revolutionary army suffered from chronic shortages of supplies. Canvas and twine were not always available, so tents were hard to come by. Officers at the rear often stopped supply wagons headed for the front to unload supplies for their own men. Some purchasing agents, furthermore, encouraged suppliers to bid up prices to increase their own commissions.[4]

These problems have not been confined to military contracts, nor even to federal contracts. The American Federation of State, County, and Municipal Employees produced a book to make a case against contractors (and to save their own jobs from contracting out). The book documents instances of fraud ranging from bribery of a Baltimore city council president for his influence in directing a sludge-hauling contract to false claims about the nutritional value and calories of frozen meals provided by private contractors for public school lunch programs.[5] Contracting thus is not the panacea its supporters claim.

Despite such troubles, contracting has increased rapidly, especially with the growth of defense spending. Contracting, furthermore, has expanded beyond military equipment to a broad range of other goods and services at all levels of government. Contracting is attractive for three reasons. First, the government, it is argued, can save money by contracting out. Private-sector companies can often pay lower salaries than civil service regulations and public employee unions would allow in the public sector. Furthermore, public choice theory contends that private-sector competition can produce public services at lower costs than would be possible in government.

Second, the government often needs goods and services that are not available in the public sector. Through contracting, the government can buy tanks without having to manage a production line. Contracting allows the government to purchase services not needed full time or to pay higher salaries than government regulations would permit. At times of severe budget cutting, many government agencies cannot increase the size of their staffs. Contracting out has become a way to hire extra workers without putting them on the regular payroll.

Finally, contracting sidesteps many governmental constraints. Contractors do not have to follow many of the same legal and constitutional standards required of government agencies, from providing equal opportunity to protecting free speech. Both government officials and contractors often rely on contracting to increase their flexibility and to avoid the normal constraints of government programs.

Since World War II in particular, governments have channeled more and more of their spending through private contractors. The growing role of the federal government in science has fueled large contracts for research and development in fields such as space exploration and pollution control. Meanwhile, state and local governments have greatly expanded their own contracting, although the full extent of their activity is impossible to measure. They continue to contract for traditional services such as road construction and have developed new agreements for the areas of planning and computer technology. They have expanded contracting in the most traditional services, such as trash

23

collection and fire and police protection. In La Mirada, California, in fact, the city government consists of only sixty regular employees. They supervise contractors who take care of everything from fire and police needs to human services and public works.[6]

The extent of the government's reliance on contractors is hard to measure over time; governments simply do not keep their books in a way that yields such data. In fiscal year 1985, though, the federal government signed more than 21.5 million contracts, totaling nearly $200 billion or 21 percent of all federal spending, according to a report distributed by the U.S. General Services Administration (a report prepared, of course, by a contractor). The Defense Department accounted for most of the spending, 82 percent of the total. Far behind was the Department of Energy (7 percent) and NASA (4 percent).[7] As Table 2-1 shows, most federal contracting is for supplies, equipment, and services. Virtually every part of government, and virtually every kind of government service, has seen a vast increase in contracting, especially since the mid-1970s. Table 2-1 presents major contracts—of more than $25,000—which represent only 2 percent of all federal contracts, but more than 91 percent of all money the federal government spent by contract. These figures have an interesting implication: the vast majority of federal contracts are small ones.

Since 1955 the federal government has moved increasingly to transfer more of the government's activities to the private sector. As one

Table 2-1 Major federal contracts by type, fiscal year 1985

	Number of contracts	Amount in billions of dollars	Percent of total
Supplies and equipment	60,976	102.7	56.2
Services	29,195	38.5	21.1
Research and development	12,074	25.7	14.1
Construction	15,540	11.5	6.3
Architects and engineers	3,004	2.0	1.1
Data processing	2,165	1.9	1.0
Property: purchase and lease	6,478	0.3	0.2
Total	129,432	182.6	100.0

Source: U.S. General Services Administration, Federal Procurement Data Center, *Federal Procurement Data System Standard Report, Fiscal Year 1985 Fourth Quarter* (Washington, D.C.: U.S. Government Printing Office, 1986).

federal policy statement argued, "The government's business is not to be in business."[8] Contracting can help lower costs and buy extra expertise, but as the Divad project painfully showed, contracts do not manage themselves. Effective contracts require careful administration, using tools often different from those used in the typical directly administered program. Without such care, disasters are likely.

The trials of Sergeant York

Early on, Army officials had christened the Divad the "Sergeant York" gun, after Alvin York, who singlehandedly defeated an entire German machine-gun battalion in World War I. Naming the gun for York was a masterful move to build public support for the gun, for no American fighting man had a greater reputation for bravery. In a battle during the Argonne Forest campaign of May 1918, then-corporal York lost half of his men in the first burst of machine-gun fire. He dug in and patiently started picking off the German gunners one by one. The Germans finally realized they were fighting only 1 man, and 6 of them charged. Using old turkey-hunting tricks he had learned in the backwoods of Tennessee, York stopped the charge and captured the German commander along with his 131 men. In the battle, Corporal York silenced 35 machine guns and killed 25 opponents. After an article in the *Saturday Evening Post* made him a national hero, he was promoted to sergeant and awarded the Congressional Medal of Honor and the French Croix de Guerre.[9]

Sergeant York was thus the perfect patron for a sharpshooting new weapon. During the 1970s, American tanks were becoming more vulnerable. The Vulcan, the gun built in the 1960s to defend them, was not powerful enough to destroy the new generation of Soviet armored aircraft. Furthermore, the all-weather fighter planes of the 1980s, equipped with advanced radar, could attack through clouds or at night. Ground-based guns aimed by human eyes were no match for these fighters. Army planners thus decided that they needed an automatic weapon: a gun that could use radar to find targets in the clouds or the dark, could aim itself and could fire projectiles with enough force to blast the planes out of the sky.

An "ultra" weapon

As military planners began designing Divad, though, another threat emerged. It was the Hind, a new Soviet missile-firing helicopter that, the U.S. military estimated, could launch its missiles from treetop level more than two-and-a-half miles away, within fifteen seconds of finding an American tank. Because antiaircraft shells would take seven seconds to reach a target that far away, Divad would have just eight seconds remaining to spot a target, move its turret, aim, and fire. Since no human being could be expected to move that fast, Army planners reasoned that the gun would need an automatic computerized control system.

The Army ended up with plans for an "ultra" weapon: a gun at the outer limits of technology. The plans called for a new ground-based unit that could outgun the best available airplane's speed, radar, and armor. The weapon was also to be used against the Soviet missile-firing helicopters. In short, the Army wanted an "all singing, all dancing weapon," as one former Pentagon official put it.[10] Divad thus reflected the desire of Pentagon planners for the very best, "cutting-edge" weapon.

The Army's critics, however, suggested that Army planners were exaggerating Soviet capabilities to justify a fancier gun for themselves. They pointed out that all-weather aircraft radars did not allow precise aiming in low visibility, especially against relatively small targets like tanks. Furthermore, many defense analysts doubted that the missile-firing helicopters would work well from treetop level far away, especially in hilly European countryside. Instead, they guessed, the helicopters would have either to draw much closer to American tanks to fire or to rise to a higher altitude. Either way the Soviet aircraft would become easier targets, and American tanks would require less ambitious guns for protection. The Army insisted on these performance criteria, however, and steered the weapon along the very edge of modern technology. Some critics noted that this decision disregarded evidence from the Vietnam War: nearly all of the 4,643 helicopters the Army lost in Vietnam were downed by rifles and machine guns.[11]

The push toward "ultra" standards is the most expensive part of any contract. As Norman R. Augustine, executive vice-president of Martin Marietta, a major defense contractor, and former undersecretary of the Army, observed, only slightly tongue in cheek, "The last ten percent of performance generates one-third of the cost and two-thirds of the problems."[12] The Army's desire to get the new system quickly drove up the cost and increased the problems. Army planners decided that, with tanks already vulnerable, they could not wait the usual decade and a half to take the new weapon system from initial design to deployment in the field. So, with the support of Congress, the Army decided to embark upon a fast-track development program called "concurrency."

Concurrency meant both buying off-the-shelf items and taking shortcuts in the acquisition process. First, the Army would keep a hands-off policy in research and development (R&D). After the Army described what it wanted, the contractor would be responsible for designing a gun to do the job. By reducing its role in R&D, the Army hoped to minimize the military's usual upgrading of requirements in the midst of design, a process that inevitably lengthened the development phase and increased the cost. Second, the Army planned to move the Divad into full production before testing was completed. Any problems that arose would, Army officials planned, be fixed along the way. In the end, though, these problems proved too big to be solved. "We knew when we started in this program that it was risky," Lt. Gen. Louis C. Wagner, Jr., the Army's deputy chief of staff said later.[13] That risk, in the end, killed the Divad.

Production problems

After an initial screening of contractors, the Army chose two firms—Ford Aerospace and General Dynamics—to prepare prototypes for a shoot-off in the spring of 1980. Neither prototype performed well in the tests. The Ford model destroyed fewer than half the targets, and its longest hit was a little more than half the range of the General Dynamics model. Furthermore, the Ford prototype's only hits were against the pilotless helicopter drones; it could not hit faster, more maneuverable airplanes.

Ford, however, won the contract. The Army adjusted the scoring of the tests to give Ford credit for a direct hit if "proximity-fused rounds"—flak shells that went off near the targets—missed by as much as forty-five feet (even though armored Soviet aircraft probably would not be brought down by a shell that missed by such a distance). Meanwhile, General Dynamics' proximity-fused shells were disqualified for not meeting regulations. These adjustments brought the scoring of the test nearly even, and the Army rated Ford's gun superior on "interoperability" with NATO forces. Ford thus won the competition. Some critics suggested that the multibillion-dollar contract was a form of bailout for Ford, which had just posted a $1.5 billion loss, the largest in corporate history. And General Dynamics, reportedly stunned at the loss of the contract, was in a weak position to fight back. Its Electric Boat Division was under investigation for overcharging the Navy for submarines.[14]

Because of the prototype's problems, however, the Army awarded Ford only a partial contract, calling for $159 million to begin production and one year to eliminate the problems.

The next year's test, however, produced a fiasco. One day, Divad critic Gregg Easterbrook explained, American and British officers gathered for a special demonstration of the Divad. Its target, a drone helicopter, hovered motionless downrange. When the crew turned on the Divad, the twin guns immediately swung toward the reviewing stand, and the VIPs dived for cover. The Army brass called for a delay to allow technicians to fix the gun. During the next attempt a few hours later, the gun pointed in the direction of the target but fired into the ground, blasting away at the weeds while the drone remained unscathed. Ford's Divad program manager later explained that, to show the gun off, the gun had been taken to the motor pool the day before the test to be washed. Water from the washing had fouled up the electronics and, according to Ford's manager, "the next day, after it dried out, it did fine." Critics predictably wondered what the gun would do on a rainy battlefield.[15]

Army officials, however, convinced themselves that the problems could be solved, and in May 1982 the Army signed a contract with Ford for 50 Divads at $6.3 million each, with an option for 226 more later.

Bogus tests

The Army was to have made the decision to order the weapon on the basis of a full operational test of the first production units. But when Ford's Divad arrived it worked so badly that, as the U.S. General Accounting Office later reported, the Army simply abandoned the tests. The radar was unreliable, the computer's graphic display sometimes failed, the ammunition system feeding the gun jammed, and the Divad did not work well in cold temperatures.[16] The *New York Times*, furthermore, reported that in other tests the first production model ignored all targets and zeroed in instead on an exhaust fan in a nearby latrine. In an editorial, the *Times* called the Divad a "high-tech, armor-plated lemon." [17]

Despite its problems, Army officials were determined to buy the Divad. Instead of canceling the weapon because it failed the tests, the Army canceled the tests. And instead of using data from the new operational tests, the Army disguised results from the Ford-General Dynamics competition as operational results. The results from the actual operational tests were not made public until November 1982, seven months after the decision to go ahead had been made.

Even Pentagon officials later severely criticized the Army's decision to sugarcoat the test results. Defense Department inspector general Joseph H. Sherick found the Army's presentation "oversimplified" and "misleading" and said it was "based on selective analysis" of the data. By the time Sherick discovered what the Army had done, though, it was too late. The Divad was already in production.[18] Army officials later conceded "some deficiencies with the system," but they promised that the problems were being resolved. More recent tests, they told a congressional committee, showed "promising progress." [19]

To strengthen their public case, furthermore, they referred to the gun more frequently as the "Sergeant York" and brought sergeants who had field-tested the gun to testify on Capitol Hill. Said one, "I believe Sergeant York is one of the most outstanding weapon systems I have ever seen, although," he admitted, "there are some minor problems." Another sergeant was more enthusiastic: "I want my system. I worked with Vulcan for five years. Forget it. Give me Sergeant York. Don't send me to do combat with the Vulcan." [20] Meanwhile, the Army decided to conduct no further tests until March 1984, a decision GAO criticized. "GAO's concern is that there will be little authenticated information as to whether Sergeant York measures up" to the Army's requirements "until two years after production has begun." [21]

The Army's reassuring words gradually evaporated as Ford's deliveries lagged months behind schedule. GAO continued to criticize the Army for failing to solve the weapon's performance problems.[22] Meanwhile, new problems surfaced. The Divad failed a cold-weather test. To make it work at all, testers in a cold chamber had to preheat its electronics for six hours. Then, in a test firing, the Divad got off only 1,354 rounds, instead of the 2,000 rounds the Army required, before breaking down.[23]

Even more serious, in tests during the summer of 1984 the Divad mistook almost half of the decoys sent against it as real targets, and when aerial attackers used electronic jamming systems the Divad could hit only one-third of the targets. It had difficulty in hitting simulated helicopters using "pop-up" techniques (hiding near treetop level, rising quickly to fire missiles, and then quickly sneaking back down among the trees). Only when the helicopter drones were outfitted with several radar reflectors to amplify the signal could the Divad hit the targets. Lieutenant General Wagner, in charge of the Army's research and development, said that the Army was "not completely satisfied," but he defended the project by saying in defensespeak, "The observed performance of the Sergeant York Gun System, operated by soldier crews, in the limited test supports the estimate of performance which led to the initial decision to initiate the materiel acquisition process." [24]

The computer tracking system continued to demonstrate serious problems. While the Divad's radar could competently track incoming planes, its computer was not very effective in aiming, especially at "jinking" airplanes—airplanes that zigzagged during attack. Lt. Gen. James Maloney, head of the Divad project, acknowledged, "No computer can handle a jinking target."[25] This was an inherent problem of any automatic aiming system. While a computer can track a plane and determine where it has been, it cannot predict precisely where it will go unless a target flies a predictable course. In aiming at maneuvering airplanes, the Divad was thus fundamentally flawed.

The introduction of new Soviet helicopters gave Army planners a chance to save Divad by changing its mission from shooting down airplanes to defending tanks against helicopters. This shift, however, posed new problems. While the Divad's computer could easily aim at a hovering target, the radar, designed for high-speed airplanes to find other high-speed airplanes, could not distinguish hovering helicopters from ground clutter. Furthermore, if the Divad did try to use its radar, the beam proved a good target for radar-seeking missiles, such as the "smart missiles" Israel used to destroy Syria's air defenses during the 1982 skirmishes in Lebanon.[26]

Divad thus was doubly cursed. Against airplanes, the radar worked, but the computer aiming system did not. Against helicopters, the computer aiming system worked, but the radar did not. The two systems combined could neither find nor shoot down targets. To counter Divad's very embarrassing test results, in one test the Army loaded targets with explosives and detonated them by remote control from the ground, to simulate what they would look like if Divad did manage to hit them.[27] When word of the faked explosions leaked out in the press, the gun came under even more vigorous attack.

The press reports enraged the Pentagon. Lieutenant General Wagner complained, "When I compared what they put in the newspapers with the data that we have gleaned from our testing, I would say it is a hatchet job." Inspector General Sherick, however, delicately dismissed the Army's complaints. "On the whole," he told a congressional committee, "I think these articles have been fairly accurate."[28] The Army nevertheless battled to keep the gun. Brig. Gen. Donald P. Whalen told House Appropriations Committee members that "the Sergeant York is a system that the Army needs for the protection of its heavy maneuvering forces very, very badly."[29] So expensive was the Divad, though, that the Army would not be able to buy enough guns to protect its tanks. So expensive was its ammunition that Divad gunners would have had to go into the field never having test-fired the weapons. Rep. Denny Smith (R-Ore.), a former fighter pilot, argued, "You'd be better off with 25 [simpler] guns than with a fancy gun like this."[30]

The Pentagon and overperformance

The Divad's "ultra" features—those designed to overcome every potential threat and to make every human judgment automatic—drove up its costs. This overspecification and overdesign resulted from the natural tendency of military planners to want the best money can buy. The problem, though, goes deeper. Edward R. Luttwak, in *The Pentagon and the Art of War*, argues that overmanagement is a product of the military's large supply of senior officers. To protect their work and their jobs, Luttwak contends, members of each service resist weapons developed by other branches. Furthermore, they often develop unique requirements that only their own weapons can meet and then, in testing, find any alternative but a home-grown device unacceptable. This, Luttwak concluded, produces "the ultimate case of too many cooks in one kitchen—or rather, of kitchens greatly enlarged to accommodate more cooks around fewer pots." [31] A special congressional study in 1985, headed by senators Barry Goldwater (R-Ariz.) and Sam Nunn (D-Ga.), similarly concluded that such interservice rivalry was a major obstacle to producing effective weapons. [32]

In Divad, the Army put aside these rivalries and agreed to use off-the-shelf components instead of designing its own system from scratch. In doing so, Army officials hoped, they would get the new gun in half the time with less cost. As Secretary Weinberger argued, "On occasions where you have a need as great as this, you do have to use all the methods you can to fill that need as quickly as possible." A slower testing process, he contended, was "a luxury of time" that the nation could not afford. [33]

During the Divad's development, however, the Army changed its mind about which threat it needed to meet—all-weather fighters or helicopters hovering at long range. It furthermore decided to go into production before the Divad had proven itself. The result was a gun that was effective against neither fighters nor helicopters. The Army spent $1.8 billion to buy 65 guns that did not work.

Cancellation of the contract was a major psychological blow to Ford Aerospace, but it did not prove to be a major financial blow—except to the 1,900 Ford workers assigned to the Divad project. The Divad contract stated that Ford would be paid for all 146 guns the Army had ordered, even though Ford had delivered only 65. Ford had already ordered many of the parts for all of the guns, but "it would be pointless now for Ford to go ahead and assemble them," Army spokesman Lt. Col. Craig MacNab said. "But we own those parts and even if we won't use the Sgt. York for anything, we may make use of the pieces." [34] It was not clear what the pieces would be used for.

General Dynamics, the loser in the Divad competition, faced a different kind of problem. In December 1985, a little more than three months after Weinberger canceled the contract, a federal grand jury indicted four General Dynamics officials for trying to defraud the government in the original competition. The day after the indictment, the Pentagon suspended General Dynamics from receiving any new federal contracts, a move that hurt the company badly. It had received $6 billion in defense contracts the year before, and more than 90 percent of that year's revenues had come from the federal government.[35]

The Pentagon's need to buy weapons, however, limited its ability to impose such harsh punishment for long. Only two companies built nuclear submarines—General Dynamics' Electric Boat Division in Connecticut and the Newport News Shipbuilding and Dry Dock Company in Virginia—and the Navy feared relying on only one. The suspension therefore was soon lifted. General Dynamics' senior officials, though, were not so lucky. James M. Beggs, who had overseen the company's Divad contract, was forced to resign as NASA administrator after being indicted. The Justice Department quietly dropped the case in June 1987 when new evidence revealed that General Dynamics' billing procedures had not been improper.

Administering contracts _____

While contracting out is a favorite prescription to reduce the size of government and to lower its costs, the Divad story shows that the issue is much more complicated. Contracting out does not necessarily provide cheap or effective goods and services.

The profit motive, as a 1986 study by the National Academy of Sciences showed, is no guarantee of high quality and low cost. The study discovered that nonprofit hospitals provided care just as good as that provided by for-profit hospitals and at a daily cost of from 3 to 10 percent less. For-profit hospitals added $470 million, the study estimated, to the nation's medical bill.[36]

There are, nevertheless, sound reasons for contracting. It would be foolish for governments to produce all the goods and services they need. They can buy everyday goods—pencils and paper, as well as trucks and bulldozers—in the market for less than they could produce them. Private-sector manufacturers can indeed achieve economies of scale that even the federal government could not hope to match. In other areas, such as local garbage collection and national park concessions, contracting has been a demonstrated success.

It is important to get past the ideological debate on government-produced services versus contracting out and to concentrate on a more useful lesson: that contracting creates its own distinctive political pressures and administrative problems. Contracting thus is not so much inherently better as it is demonstrably different from the direct provision of services by governments themselves. Those differences hinge on three key problems: on setting standards and deciding on the contract's goals; on creating genuine competition; and on effectively overseeing the contractor's performance by collecting accurate feedback.

Setting standards

Contracts are possible only if the government can define what it wants to buy in a way that clearly tells a contractor what is expected. Sometimes, for low-tech, off-the-shelf items such as paperclips and even automobiles, that is an easy task. The same is true of services such as garbage collection, where the signs of bad performance are unmistakable. In these goods and services, it is relatively simple to define what the government wants to buy, to bid on a contract, and to determine later if the good or service actually is delivered.

Even for common items, however, contract specifications can be voluminous. For example, Military Specification MIL-F-1499F, amended in 1980, is eighteen pages long. It sets forth in excruciating detail the requirements for fruitcakes that the Pentagon buys for its troops. The cook, for example, is instructed to "examine each ingredient organoleptically" (that is, by means of sensory organs, according to the dictionary). "I assume this means that we are to lick the beaters and the bowl," quipped Senator Nunn. The nuts are to "be from one-eighth to three-eighths inches" in size and the raisins "shall be soda dipped or bleached Thompson seedless, select size" that "may be soaked as necessary to prevent clumping." [37] Such regulations might seem ridiculous, and indeed they are excessively detailed. However, government officials point out, careful specifications ensure that the government gets what it pays for—that, for example, a contractor does not deliver sawdust mixed with dried fruit and call it fruitcake.

When government's needs range beyond the ordinary, the process gets even more complicated. Government often is called upon to produce goods and services precisely because the private sector cannot or will not. That means that government must often rely on contractors to help design the goods before it can buy them. This, in turn, upsets the conventional logic of contracting, which assumes that potential suppliers compete in supplying goods of high quality at low prices. (Many

33

weapons systems, in fact, are produced in "GOCO"—government-owned, contractor-operated—factories in which the government itself assumes much of the risk.) Thus, government contracting often transforms the producer-consumer relationship of traditional contracts into a difficult partnership, in which the contractor and the government work together to define what is to be bought. Three major problems— goldplating, overspecification, and overregulation—compound the difficulties, especially in military contracts.

Goldplating. As Luttwak argued, the very existence of large and separate bureaucracies—Army, Air Force, Navy, and Marines—leads to the creation of highly specialized and sometimes overengineered weapons. Goldplating, as the Goldwater-Nunn study explained, means "giving a system more capability or additional capabilities than are required to meet the threat."[38] The military design and testing bureaucracies naturally have a tendency to be creative, to imagine the most dangerous threat its forces might face, and to design weapons to counter every possibility. However, the resulting weapons are often theoretical masterpieces that have enormous difficulty performing consistently in the rigors and uncertainties of the battlefield.

The Army had many simpler alternatives to the Divad, including a "light" Divad towed by a truck and a smaller and lighter General Dynamics model with a laser range finder instead of the Divad's radar system. General Electric also developed a much cheaper gun that could fire seven times as many shells per minute as the Divad, for half the price. The Army found the gun unacceptable, however, because while it did very well over most conditions it would face, its performance slipped at the very outer reaches of the threat Army planners defined. Because it was less effective outside a two-and-a-half mile range, the General Electric model was rejected, even though some analysts questioned how effective Soviet helicopters would be beyond that range in rolling European terrain.[39]

Goals often change during the term of the contract. Army planners first defined the Divad gun's goal as shooting down all-weather jets, then shifted to missile-firing helicopters. They insisted on a gun that would hit targets more than two-and-a-half miles away, a distance beyond the range of most automatically controlled ground guns. The planners designed so many requirements into the gun that in the end it did not work at all. "We've finally found a way to make a gun more expensive than a missile," complained one recently retired colonel.[40]

As a result of this design process, much military equipment is almost unbelievably complicated. The Air Force's F15 Eagle fighter contains 585,000 parts, 4,200 feet of tubing, and 20 miles of wiring. One McDonnell Douglas foreman who supervises the construction of the plane defined the F15 as "a collection of parts flying in very close formation." [41] Such complicated equipment is the inevitable result of ever more ambitious weapons planning, which in turn can be traced to increasingly more sophisticated Soviet weapons as well as to the temptation for goldplating. Goldplating, furthermore, is not restricted to military hardware. It is a natural tendency that develops when a partnership replaces competition in the buyer-producer relationship, when government and private contractors collaborate in producing goods. We will return to that point shortly.

Overspecification. Overspecification means writing unnecessarily detailed guidelines for a contract. A plastic whistle purchased by the military, for example, comes with sixteen single-spaced pages of specifications, covering everything from the little cork ball inside the whistle to the authorized tissue wrapping paper. The details, contained in military specifications labeled MIL-W-1053F, spell out everything—and more—anyone could want to know about making and buying a whistle. Military planners maintain that the details in the specifications must be airtight to ensure that the military gets what it pays for, that suppliers do not substitute inferior goods.[42] Critics wonder why the military cannot simply buy the whistles stocked by sporting-good stores.

In another case, investigators discovered that the Air Force was charging the government $748 for a pair of duckbill pliers that a government engineer found in a hardware store for $7.61.[43] The hardware-store model was exactly the same, except for a small notch on one end, a special black finish, and an Air Force parts number engraved on the side. When the engineer pointed out the difference, the supplier, Boeing, slashed the price to $90 and added a new charge of $95,307 for "support equipment management." The total price of the tools went from $557,500 to exactly $557,500.

An Air Force spokesman said that ordinary hardware-store pliers would not work in the job for which the special pliers were designed: positioning a small pin in a KC135 jet tanker's engine. The special notch was important for holding the pin. "Anyone who has tried to perform minor maintenance on their car or kitchen sink knows that lack of the proper tool can make a simple task impossible," the spokesman explained, although the Air Force admitted that "there was an appearance of overpricing." The real cost of the pliers was a small fraction of Boeing's charge to the Pentagon. The company's original proposal of $5,096 for two pairs of pliers included $305 for the two pairs and

35

Boeing's surcharge for buying them from a subcontractor. The remaining $4,791 was for additional "management support tasks and profit," which covered management, financial controls, purchasing of materials, costs analyses, planning, computing time, fringe benefits, and other items. These items are a standard part of every contract and are included regardless of a contract's size. The larger the contract, the smaller the percentage devoted to such "support tasks."

While the Air Force eventually bargained Boeing down to $1,494 for two pairs of pliers—a 70 percent reduction—the case illustrates the problem of overspecification. When the Air Force said the supplier would have to cut a small notch on regular pliers, that it needed only two pairs, and that the supplier needed to meet many pages of related requirements, the cost increased a hundred times. Multiplied over and over again through the thousands and thousands of contracts the Pentagon annually signs, overspecification enormously increases the Defense budget. It undoubtedly increases the cost of contracts in other government agencies as well.

Overregulation. An enormous number of rules and specifications governs the production of materials in government contracts. Contractors must keep their books in prescribed ways, and they must agree not to discriminate in hiring and not to spoil the environment with industrial wastes, among many other requirements. The specifications for one military aircraft range over 24,000 documents. One document covering electronic parts refers to 255 other documents, which in turn refer to 1,374 more, of which half are more than ten years old. To follow the rules means designing obsolete electronic components into the most up-to-date equipment.[44]

The reams of military specifications—MILSPECS for short—exist for good reasons. Military equipment must work over a far broader and less predictable range of conditions than civilian versions. Commercial airlines do not buy planes to fly into steaming jungles or the frozen Arctic, but the military cannot risk having its transport planes or other equipment break down in the middle of a war because of weather extremes. Similarly, the government cannot countenance discrimination by race or sex or religion by those who receive government money. Public policy demands that firms receiving governmental contracts comply with pollution control rules. Government auditors cannot do their job if creative corporate accounting masks the way contractors spend government money.

However, overregulation is fundamentally rooted in a dual pathology. First, government suffers from the dysfunctional tendency of bureaucracies to overspecify requirements for goods and services, which in turn leads to overregulation to ensure that those requirements are met. Government's reflexive response to problems is a related disorder. When problems arise—as inevitably they do, from honest mistakes or attempts at fraud—the response of legislators and interest groups is often to pressure administrators to make sure the problems never recur. That means writing rules to combat abuses. Over time these regulations accumulate. The paradoxical result is that programs contracted out to reduce the size and scope of governmental action often become even more encrusted with governmental controls.

If contracting out is to be successful, therefore, the government must specify what it wants to buy in enough detail so the contractor knows what is required (and so the government can determine later if the job gets done), but not in so much detail that the contractor becomes hamstrung—or rings up high costs in compliance that the taxpayer in the end must pay.

Creating competition

As a means for providing the best services at the lowest costs, contracting requires competition. Competition in contracting simulates the market, where consumers shop around for the best bargain before deciding what to buy. However, the stark fact about contracting, especially in the federal government, is that there is very little competition: fewer than half of all federal contracts are awarded after competitive bids. In fiscal year 1985, bidding competition preceded only 44 percent of all contracts.[45] The pool of willing and reliable contractors for many services, even at the state and local level, is often small.[46]

Indeed, as the Navy's Competition Advocate General, Rear Adm. Stuart F. Platt, explained, "There's an institutional bias against competition" in the military. In 1985 the ten largest defense contractors accounted for nearly 35 percent of military spending, up from 29 percent in 1980.[47] The reasons are both strategic and political. In many cases, the weapons are so complicated that few potential manufacturers exist. Most manufacturers would be unwilling to build the huge plants the weapons require without some assurance that their investments would be rewarded. The armed services, for their part, struggle to keep contractors in business, for they cannot afford to have their production options limited, especially in case of war. The result is a mutually supporting relationship that former president Dwight D. Eisenhower, in his farewell address in 1961, called the "military-industrial complex."

Many government contractors, inside and outside the defense

37

industry, are protected against substantial competition. A very large number of contracts are awarded without competitive bids. When they win military contracts, some contractors are supplied with military equipment and factories, which saves them substantial money and lowers their risk. Even losing bidders are often protected so they will remain in the pool of future suppliers. And, as the Divad case illustrates, many contracts contain generous cancellation clauses to avoid discouraging potential contractors from entering the business.

As a result, competition in government contracting is often artificial. The further goods and services go from traditional off-the-shelf items, the less competition there is. It becomes harder to write specifications; it is more difficult to find many competent bidders; and contractors are willing to take less risk. Most big contractors, especially in defense, dominate their markets; they are monopolies that sell to only one buyer, the government.

The lack of competition does little to promote quality or cost consciousness. A Pentagon survey, in fact, showed that most companies needed two to ten times longer to complete a project than their own engineers had projected as necessary. Most programs averaged efficiency at less than 50 percent of the projected standard.[48] At the same time, a Navy study showed that defense work was up to ten times more lucrative than contracts for the private sector. In 1983, for example, Boeing reported a profit of $98 million on $7 billion of commercial sales. In its military contracts, there was almost three times more profit—$289 million—on $2.6 billion in sales.[49] And during the 1980-1983 recession defense contractors' profits averaged 4.70 percent per year, compared to all similar manufacturers' average annual *loss* of 3.65 percent, according to a *Washington Post* study.[50]

While nearly everyone worships competition in theory, in practice most people seek to minimize their risks, at least in the short run, and maximize their certainties. Real competition produces one winner and a host of losers. After a contract is awarded, the winning contractor often feels heavy pressure to please the government and to avoid losing the contract. In government competition, the hiring agency cannot risk losing its few suppliers, so the competition is skewed. Thus, there typically is relatively little competition to begin with, the losers often do not suffer seriously, and the winner is often more driven to protect the contract than to take risks for high performance.

Furthermore, competition itself often competes with other goals. There are inevitably pressures for broad distribution of government money and for widespread participation in the administration of government programs. Government programs, for example, seek to ensure that small businesses and minority firms get a share of the contracts. Government contracts, of course, have also long been a source of corruption, especially at the state and local level, where bid rigging and kickbacks have fueled many political campaigns. The efficiency that competition is meant to promote often in practice loses out to other important (and sometimes illegal) goals.

Overseeing performance

The first trickle of horror stories about defense procurement in the 1980s quickly led to more investigations and a flood of reports of even more abuses. In 1987 the Pentagon was investigating 59 of the nation's top 100 defense contractors for violations, many of which involved costs wrongly applied to defense projects. Other complaints ranged from illegal payments to military officers and political candidates to falsification of performance records and bid rigging. The Defense Department responded by increasing its punishment of the guilty. From October 1985 through March 1986, the Pentagon barred 417 contractors from receiving further contracts, an increase from 178 during the same period in 1983-1984.[51]

Substantial evidence of shoddy work surfaced as well. Al Lovelace, vice-president in charge of productivity at General Dynamics, estimated in 1984 that about 15 percent of money spent on military procurement—about $15 billion—purchased unacceptable products that had to be scrapped and remanufactured. Paul Thayer, former deputy secretary of defense, contended that inferior work added from 10 to 30 percent to the cost of military equipment.[52]

Despite the problems of corruption and poor performance, however, it remains hard for government to impose meaningful penalties. Cancellation of a contract, the only real penalty for bad performance, is a measure so severe that the pressures to avoid it are great. If invoked, this punishment hurts the government as well, leaving officials with the job of finding new producers and running a new competition. Even with readily available goods and services, such as pencils or garbage collection, government must incur substantial delay and additional costs in setting up a new bidding process. For more advanced goods, such as weapon systems, there may be few alternatives. As one military officer complained, "It would be swell if I could say, 'You're a naughty boy and I'm going to cast you into oblivion.' But if I do, where am I going to buy the submarines and tanks and planes that I need?" [53]

The challenge is making the punishment fit the crime, strong enough to be effective yet not so extreme as to be unthinkable.[54] Making the punishment stick is another difficulty. The Pentagon suspended one contractor sentenced to six months in jail for selling the Army $28,000 of military equipment that did not exist. He nevertheless continued to do business from jail and later on probation, through a shadow company operated by his son and daughter. Another suspended contractor used four different corporations to get thirty-six military contracts before finally being caught and then sentenced to fifteen years in jail for fraud. The Defense Department's lists of suspended contractors are often months out of date, and apparently no one checks those listed to see if they are still in business. Shady contractors are also getting more skillful in avoiding penalties. "Their side is getting smarter," one Pentagon watchdog explained.[55]

At the same time, many contractors complain about oversight overkill. Sanford N. McDonnell, head of McDonnell Douglas, accused the federal government of "over-managing, over-specifying, over-scrutinizing" the work of defense contractors. He cited tens of thousands of days occupied by visits from thousands of government auditors. "The overwhelming load of all this just drives you up the wall," he complained. Oversight overkill and overspecification together produce mountains of requirements that contractors must meet. "There's a lot of garbage in these documents," another McDonnell Douglas official said, "and nobody can read all of that. So some people get sloppy in their attitude toward requirements." [56]

Micromanagement and good management ———

The predictable reaction to such problems is more congressional investigation and more public demands that the problems stop. Congress, especially since 1983, has engaged in more micromanagement of the Pentagon and its programs. Each year from 1983 to 1986, Congress added 115 new directives to the Defense Department, compared with an average of only 36 per year from 1970 to 1982. Reports and studies required by Congress increased to 88 per year from 1983 to 1986, compared with 14 per year during the earlier period.[57] Congress has demanded studies on even such minute things as military jacket linings and Hawaiian milk.[58]

Well-publicized problems drive Congress to try to micromanage the Pentagon, and the Pentagon's own efforts to improve contract management have added pages of military specifications and unleashed legions of auditors upon contractors. This is all scarcely surprising. Stories in the media have a remarkable tendency to focus public attention and shape the policy agenda. They dominate the news and become vivid symbols demanding immediate answers.

The inevitable result is micromanagement: centralization of administrative details, through rules and audits, through congressional directives and demands for information. The irony of such centralization is that it develops as the result of the government's effort to *decentralize* its operations, to delegate more responsibility to the private sector, and to reduce its size and scope. Management of details thus is often left in the hands of those who produce and examine the rules and data, technocrats within contracting companies and government agencies. Hence, the key decisions about broad policy often get lost in the details of micromanagement.

Sharing power

Contracting thus is scarcely a trouble-free governmental strategy. Contract goals are often hard to write and competitive bidding is often elusive. Contractors sometimes are skilled at what is known as the "camel's nose" approach. Once a camel sticks his nose under a tent, it is hard to keep the rest of the animal outside. Similarly, contractors, knowing that the government has limited options, sometimes underbid to win a contract. Once the government awards a contract, furthermore, ensuring good performance requires great vigilance. Finding out what contractors are actually doing with the public money is very often a daunting task.

When problems occur, therefore, micromanagement becomes an especially attractive approach to curing contracting problems. If a contractor tries to sneak inferior ingredients into a fruitcake, the government is tempted to stipulate, in great detail, how to make it. To be sure, knowing that Congress or the Pentagon might oversee the smallest details of a contract keeps contractors on their toes. Micromanagement, however, does not solve the broader problems of contracting because it approaches them from the wrong level. Government contracting is not problematic because of inadequate regulation of details but because of the fundamental problems of meshing the public and private sectors.

The growth of contracting has blurred the lines dividing public from private. The structures and policies of corporations that deal heavily with government have diverged greatly from those of corporations doing business principally with other industries or with consumers. The government has become involved in key decisions for these firms—decisions about the most fundamental matters such as what they

41

will produce and how they will do so. At the same time, the government and the public interest have become more dependent on private behavior. From national defense to garbage collection, areas affecting the quality of life in the United States have become a matter of intermingled public and private interests.

The central issue thus is about values—about how to mesh often different public and private values into a smoothly functioning system and how to achieve this result without sacrificing the public interest. In the process, contracting has become less a device of competition than of accommodation, of bargaining and negotiation about the terms of public-private ties. Some of this accommodation concerns the *what* of public programs. There is a powerful pressure in contracted-out programs for the contractor's goals to become the government's goals. It is tempting for the government to want to buy what the contractor wants to sell. Indeed, the close relationships among contracting experts, both in and out of government, make it ever more difficult to make the government's goals paramount. Those public goals must nonetheless remain central as the government seeks to create incentives for a cooperative relationship with private contractors.

The accommodation involves as well the *how* of governmental programs. Contracting might well increase the efficiency of government programs. However, it can substantially change the basic rights that Americans have come to rely on and that are normally provided in governmentally administered programs. The Fourteenth Amendment to the U.S. Constitution guarantees due process in providing government services, while the First Amendment guarantees free speech. As the Supreme Court has interpreted the law, recipients of government programs operated under contract often lose rights that they would have enjoyed had the provision of services remained with the government. When goods and services are provided by contract, there is no guarantee of equal protection in service provision; and "whistle blower" protection for public employees who use their right to free speech to challenge government actions does not apply to employees of contractors.

Micromanagement thus attacks the problem of contracting at the wrong level. Managing contracts is not a problem of controlling details. Rather, it is fundamentally a problem of reconciling values, public and private, and developing a smoothly functioning system that seeks efficiency without sacrificing the broader public interest.

Ruth DeHoog has argued that "contracting out does not mimic the market, and it creates additional bureaucratic problems." [59] Agreeing on the contract standards, measuring the performance of the contractors, and judging and enforcing outcomes are the critical points at which these problems occur. If there are additional bureaucratic problems, new administrative strategies must come into play. As the Army's VIABLE project shows, success is indeed possible.

VIABLE and computer management

By the late 1970s, the Army was plagued by an obsolete computer system, a system that could not run modern software and that constantly broke down. Neither could it keep up with the growing volume of logistical details, including personnel, payroll, and supply records, that Army officials needed to process. In 1977, therefore, the Army launched Project VIABLE: the Vertical Installation Automation Baseline system, a tribute both to the Army's planning and its unfailing ability to come up with catchy acronyms.[60]

VIABLE was to be a new system designed to connect the various Army commands with bases—and more than 18,000 computer terminals—scattered around the country. (Hence the "vertical installation" in its name, for it was to tie headquarters vertically to Army installations.) VIABLE was unlike any computer acquisition project the Pentagon had conducted before. It was one of the largest electronic data processing contracts ever awarded, and even more important, VIABLE was the military's first effort to use a streamlined procurement process in buying computers. Instead of following the usual procedure of engineering the system and identifying in detail all of the components for the potential contractor, the Army instead carefully defined what the system would have to do and then left the details up to the contractor. That, Army officials hoped, would encourage contractors to use off-the-shelf, commercially available equipment and therefore save time and money. Of course, this was the theory behind "concurrency" in the Divad program. This time the theory worked.

The Army worked for four years shaping the description of its requirements, a task that proved the most difficult part of the process. The staff began with little information about the Army's workload, its data processing needs, and the configuration of each facility where VIABLE would be installed. What information there was about the forty-seven Army installations involved was haphazard and unorganized. The first step in preparing to draw up the contract therefore was to update the Army's internal management.

Defining the requirements for performance in advance was quite different from the Army's old way of doing business, in which the Army would set specifications at the beginning but then negotiate with the contractor as work progressed. When asked to spell out their performance needs, Army staff around the country tended to respond in the old patterns, so that substantial retraining was needed in the process of drawing up the requirements. The specifications were eventually modified eighteen times over the fifteen-month period of competition for the contract.

Three years later, Electronic Data Systems, the winning contractor, delivered the new computer system ahead of schedule, within budget, and without protest. The Army saved $250 million over what the conventional procurement system would have spent, and it got an innovative, state-of-the-art system designed to serve its needs for years into the future. Managers got more accurate information than the traditional procurement system would have allowed and employees got solid training for their computer tasks. Project VIABLE, in short, proved a huge success, especially when compared with an Air Force purchase of a computer system that suffered from all of the conventional problems.

Two features separated VIABLE from failures such as the Divad project. First, the Army's planners very carefully established—in advance—the specifications for their new computer system. They talked to the people who would use it, they examined their facilities, and they went through a multistep process of sharpening the system's criteria— all before they let the contract. VIABLE's specifications represented a carefully bargained set of goals to meet the Army's needs. In the Divad case, on the other hand, the process of defining the specifications never did end. The Army continued to produce new criteria, both to meet changing perceptions of their needs and to circumvent production problems as they surfaced.

Second, Army planners were careful to take VIABLE to the state of the art, but not beyond it. The computer system was one that any other organization could have purchased. In Divad, on the other hand, Army engineers tried to design a gun to do things that no gun had ever done before. That in turn brought extra risks that the Army was not able to circumvent. This is not to say that the government must avoid reaching beyond current capabilities when signing contracts, because the government has a legitimate role in promoting revolutionary research and development. The Pentagon has an important interest in continuing to push back the cutting edge, and it often is the sole buyer of advanced weapons. But it is not always necessary to go beyond conventional technology. And when government contracts push the edge of possibility, they must be managed as the experiments they are. The Army's chief mistake in Divad was to design an entirely new gun and to push it into production as if it were a proven piece of equipment.

The secret of efficiency and effectiveness thus does not lie simply in contracting out. Instead, the solution lies in the way contracts are *managed*. Good contract management means concentration on policy goals instead of details, focusing on performance by the contractor instead of the procedures followed. The government has a legitimate interest in ensuring, for example, that contractors do not discriminate or spoil the environment. In the long run, though, government officials—whether members of Congress or program administrators—do a disservice by involving themselves too deeply in the details of a program at the expense of attention to its overall policy aims. That is the lesson of Divad's failure and VIABLE's success.

Notes _____

1. *Washington Post*, June 4, 1985, A1.
2. *Washington Post*, August 28, 1985, A1.
3. U.S. Comptroller General, *Sergeant York: Concerns About the Army's Accelerated Acquisition Strategy* (Washington, D.C.: U.S. General Accounting Office, 1986), Report NSIAD-86-89, 405.
4. Erna Risch, *Supplying Washington's Army* (Washington, D.C.: U.S. Government Printing Office, 1981).
5. American Federation of State, County, and Municipal Employees, *Passing the Bucks* (Washington, D.C.: AFSCME, 1984), 38-39, 72.
6. *National Journal*, March 1, 1986, 504.
7. U.S. General Services Administration Federal Procurement Data System, *Federal Procurement Data System Standard Report, Fiscal Year 1985 Fourth Quarter* (Washington, D.C.: U.S. Government Printing Office, 1986).
8. U.S. Office of Management and Budget, Circular A-76, revised March 29, 1979, 2.
9. David Lee, "Alvin Callum York," in *Dictionary of Military Biography*, ed. Roger J. Spiller (Westport, Conn.: Greenwood Press, 1984), III:1219-1220.
10. Gregg Easterbrook, "Why Divad Wouldn't Die," *Washington Monthly*, November 1984, 13.
11. Gregg Easterbrook, "Divad," *Atlantic Monthly*, October 1982, 31-33.
12. Norman R. Augustine, *Augustine's Laws* (New York: Vintage, 1986), 107.
13. U.S. Congress, Senate, Committee on Armed Services, *Oversight on the Division Air Defense Gun System (Divad)*, hearings, 98th Cong., 2d sess., 1984, 33.
14. Easterbrook, "Divad," 34-36.
15. Ibid., 37; Easterbrook, "Why Divad Wouldn't Die."
16. U.S. Comptroller General, *The Army Should Confirm Sergeant York Air Defense Gun's Reliability and Maintainability Before Exercising Next Production Option* (Washington, D.C.: U.S. General Accounting Office, 1983), MASAD-83-8, i.
17. *New York Times*, March 7, 1984, A22.
18. U.S. Congress, Senate, Committee on Governmental Affairs, *Management of the Department of Defense: Part 9*, hearings, 98th Cong., 2d sess., 1984, 6-8.

19. U.S. Congress, House of Representatives, Committee on Appropriations, *Department of Defense Appropriations for 1985: Part 4*, hearings, 98th Cong., 2d sess., 1984, 473, 493-494.
20. Senate Armed Services Committee, *Oversight on the Divad*, 55.
21. Comptroller General, *The Army Should Confirm*, ii, v.
22. Ibid, iii.
23. *Washington Post*, March 6, 1985, A7.
24. Senate Armed Services Committee, *Oversight on the Divad*, 18, 37-38.
25. Quoted by Easterbrook, "Why Divad Wouldn't Die," 14.
26. Ibid., 14-15; Easterbrook, "Divad," 38.
27. Gregg Easterbrook, "York, York, York," *New Republic*, December 30, 1985, 17.
28. Senate Armed Services Committee, *Oversight on the Divad*, 48, 61-62.
29. House Appropriations Committee, *DoD Appropriations*, 475.
30. Quoted in *Business Week*, August 6, 1984, 28.
31. Edward N. Luttwak, *The Pentagon and the Art of War* (New York: Simon & Schuster, 1984), 166, 182-183, 184.
32. U.S. Congress, Senate, Committee on Armed Services, *Defense Organization: The Need for Change*, staff report, 99th Cong., 1st sess., 1985, 540.
33. Quoted in *Los Angeles Times*, August 29, 1985, part I, 6.
34. Ibid, part IV, 1.
35. *Washington Post*, December 3, 1985, A1; December 4, 1985, A11.
36. Bradford H. Gray and Walter J. McNerney, "For-Profit Enterprise in Health Care," *New England Journal of Medicine* 314 (June 5, 1986): 1325; *Washington Post*, June 5, 1986, A10.
37. U.S. Congress, Senate, *Congressional Record*, 99th Cong., 1st sess., December 19, 1985, S18167-71.
38. Senate Armed Services Committee, *Defense Organization*, 558.
39. Easterbrook, "Divad," 39.
40. Quoted in ibid., 30.
41. Quoted in *New York Times*, June 15, 1986, Sec. 3, 4.
42. *Washington Post*, May 20, 1985, A1.
43. The case comes from the *Washington Post*, March 22, 1985, A1.
44. *New York Times*, June 15, 1986, Sec. 3, 4.
45. General Services Administration, *Federal Procurement Data System*.
46. Ruth Hoogland DeHoog, *Contracting Out for Human Services* (Albany: State University of New York, 1984), 67-68.
47. *New York Times*, May 12, 1985, Sec. 3, 1.
48. *New York Times*, March 31, 1985, Sec. 1, 1.
49. *Washington Post*, April 1, 1985, A6.
50. *Washington Post*, August 7, 1985, A2.
51. *New York Times*, June 15, 1986, Sec. 3, 4.
52. *New York Times*, July 8, 1984, Sec. 3, 4.
53. *New York Times*, June 15, 1986, Sec. 3, 4.
54. For a discussion, see Bruce L. R. Smith, "Accountability and Independence in the Contract State," in *The Dilemma of Accountability in Modern Government*, ed. Bruce L. R. Smith and D. C. Hague, (New York: St. Martin's Press, 1975), 1-45.
55. *Wall Street Journal*, May 6, 1986, 23.
56. *New York Times*, June 15, 1986, Sec. 3, 4.

46

57. U.S. Comptroller General, *Congressional Requests for Information on Defense Activities* (Washington, D.C.: U.S. General Accounting Office, 1986), NSIAD-86-65BR, 6.
58. *Washington Post*, July 4, 1985, A1.
59. DeHoog, *Contracting Out for Human Services*, 136.
60. The case comes from Charlotte Jean Lakey, "Acquisition Management: Applicability of OMB Circular A-109 for Commercially Available Automatic Data Processing Resources," Master of Arts thesis, Department of Government and Foreign Affairs, University of Virginia, 1986.

Grants: a partnership for community development 3

With great fanfare, Congress in 1974 passed the Community Development Block Grant Program, part of the Nixon administration's ambitious strategy for loosening the strings on federal aid and returning substantial power to local governments for deciding how federal money ought to be spent. Yet scarcely two years later, the Southern Regional Council, a public interest lobby in Atlanta, was calling the CD program a "waste—a squandering of public money." Local governments, the council wrote, "have been permitted to deviate at will from the national responsibilities that the 1974 act supposedly places on them." One city built tennis courts in what the council said was an affluent neighborhood. Another community upgraded a road that, according to its mayor, was used by "hundreds of people who go to and from the country club section every day." These projects and many others like them, Peter J. Petkas, the council's director, told a Senate committee, "were a flagrant misuse of millions of tax dollars intended to fight urban blight and improve the living conditions of the poor city dwellers."[1]

Congress had given communities a wide berth in directing their programs. Because they were closer to the people, local groups could presumably pursue projects that would better meet their citizens' needs than projects planned by bureaucrats far away in Washington. These hopes, however, clashed with the harsh reality of local politics. Given both federal cash and local choice, local officials faced severe pressures to distribute the money widely around their cities. Although many federal officials—both in Congress and in the Department of Housing

49

and Urban Development (HUD), which administered the program—had vague and differing expectations for the program, they were not pleased with the early reports of money siphoned from the poor. These reports, reinforced by the earlier disenchantment with the Department of Labor's infamous job training program, CETA (Comprehensive Employment and Training Act), weakened federal enthusiasm for relying on state and local governments to administer federal programs.

A history of federal grants ⸻

Intergovernmental grants date from the first years of the American Republic. As the federal government began dividing the western lands after the Revolutionary War—when the "West" was Ohio—it set aside one portion of every parcel to be sold to support local education in the territory. Such land grants continued through the nineteenth century and later provided the foundation for land-grant universities in each of the states. Cash grants were rarer, although when the federal government built a politically embarrassing surplus in 1837, it distributed cash grants to each state. (That was the first and last time the federal government encountered *that* problem, even though the general revenue-sharing program, enacted by Congress in 1972, first emerged as a plan to spend a projected federal surplus from the end of the Vietnam War. The surplus, of course, never materialized.)

The New Deal under President Franklin D. Roosevelt forever changed American intergovernmental relations. The federal government began making much larger grants covering a far broader range of activities. It was, as Jane Perry Clark Carey wrote in 1938, "the rise of a new federalism." [2] This dramatic growth in federal activity in what formerly had been the principal responsibilities of state and local governments had two roots. First, critics complained that state and local governments had become administratively incompetent and politically irresponsible. The states' boundaries were often illogical, too large for responsive government and too small for comprehensive attack on regional problems. Political corruption hampered local governments, while their small jurisdictions produced a fragmented approach to solving their problems. Second, neither the states nor the local governments had the financial means to meet the problems within their boundaries, as the Depression illustrated all too painfully.

The New Deal created a wave of intergovernmental programs, funded by the federal government but administered by state and local agents. After World War II, intergovernmental grant programs increasingly became the instrument of choice for many federal domestic programs. Starting in the late 1950s, federal aid to state governments built the interstate highway system, and during the 1960s federal grants helped rebuild urban slums to provide the poor with basic services.

Many of these programs enabled state and local governments to expand their traditional functions, such as transportation and education. Many more, however, were designed to induce states and local governments to do what the federal government wanted done—to serve as administrative agents for federal programs and their national goals. Federal grants, then, are a product of the nation's constitutional system. The "reserved powers" clause of the Constitution, embodied in the Tenth Amendment, reserves to the states all powers not directly given to the federal government. The Constitution thereby makes it impossible for the federal government to command action by state and local governments. (The notable exception is protection of constitutionally guaranteed rights through the federal judicial system, a protection that gives the federal government enormous leverage over state and local activities.) Furthermore, the overwhelming complexity of the federal government and the enormous size of the country make it impossible to administer the nation effectively from Washington. Even if it could be done, the rich American tradition of self-government would stand in the way of an all-powerful national government.

The federal government thus faced a quandary that was especially acute in the post-World War II years. State and local governments needed financial and administrative help, as problems ranging from inadequate roads to the needs of the poor grew. At the same time constitutional, administrative, and traditional restraints hindered direct federal action. The growth of federal grants was a special adaptation to these problems. By creating grants the federal government could channel money to those programs—and to those regions—that most needed it. The federal money was usually well-nigh irresistible. (The interstate highway system, for example, required state governments to contribute only 10 cents for every dollar of construction costs.) At the same time, the federal government could insist that state and local governments meet certain requirements as conditions for the money. Grants thus created a special federal-state-local partnership that overcame the obstacles to federal action, a partnership that was cemented by the lure of federal money but that carried with it a package of federal requirements. State and local governments became agents of federal policy without surrendering the fundamental autonomy at the core of the American system.

51

The growth of federal aid _____

Federal aid grew through the Eisenhower years with the beginning of urban renewal and the interstate highway system. The war on poverty during the presidency of Lyndon B. Johnson further expanded aid into social programs. Federal aid grew very rapidly during the 1970s, more because of the generosity of Congress than because of the domestic policies of Richard Nixon and Gerald R. Ford. Federal aid continued to grow at a rapid rate until the Carter administration, when in 1978 it reached its highest point in American history. Federal aid to state and local governments then accounted for 17 percent of all federal spending and contributed 27 percent of all state and local expenditures. Put differently, the federal government supplied more than $1 for every $3 state and local governments raised on their own.[3] With the first Carter budget cuts, and later with Ronald Reagan's assault on domestic spending, federal aid dropped sharply, until it resumed its upward course—at a much slower rate—in 1983. (See Figure 3-1.) Federal grants thus stabilized in the 1980s at a lower but still significant share of federal spending.

Nearly half of all these grants—46 percent in fiscal year 1985—goes through state and local governments for payments to individuals. The largest of these income transfer programs is medicaid, which provides medical services for the poor; other important intergovernmental transfer programs include aid for dependent children (the federal component of welfare), subsidized housing, and child nutrition programs. As the formulas and eligibility standards for these programs drive up their cost, and as discretionary programs such as job training and community development programs suffer cuts, payments to individuals are becoming the largest part of federal aid.

In short, about half of federal aid goes for projects such as community development and highways, and the other half goes for income transfer programs for individuals.

In both kinds of programs, state and local governments act as the federal government's administrative agents. In the first type, though, these governments do the work. In the second, they pass the money through to others—individuals or service providers—who are responsible for the services. The result is a tremendously complex system, founded on the enduring push to maximize state and local autonomy while pursuing federal goals.

These goals, moreover, have grown substantially beyond the aims of the individual programs. Because the federal government's direct control over state and local governments is so limited, piggybacking

Figure 3-1   Federal grants to state and local governments, 1940-1985 (in billions of constant 1982 dollars)

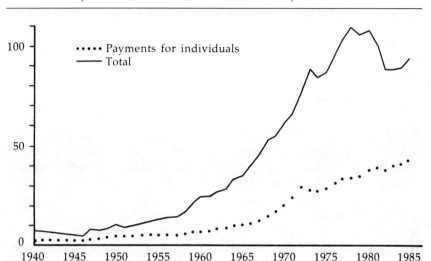

Source: U.S. Office of Management and Budget, *Budget of the United States Government, Historical Tables, Fiscal Year 1987* (Washington, D.C.: U.S. Government Printing Office, 1986).

unrelated requirements onto grants has been an appealing way to promote federal goals.

Some of these requirements are direct orders—for instance, federal standards mandating equal employment opportunity or forbidding the dumping of raw sewage into the ocean. Others are crosscutting rules, such as federal civil rights requirements that apply to all aid programs. Still other rules are crossover sanctions, in which the federal government threatens to apply sanctions (for instance, the cutoff of federal highway aid) if state or local governments do not meet separate requirements (such as enforcement of a 55-mile-per-hour speed limit). Finally, some federal regulations are partial preemptions. For example, if a state does not meet the water quality standards set by the U.S. Environmental Protection Agency, the federal government will step in and enforce the rules itself.[4]

These developments have created a complex system of subsidies and regulations layered over the network of more than 75,000 federal, state, local, and special district governments in the country. The intergovernmental system in many ways becomes a magnet for the nation's domestic hopes and ambitions. In the process, however, the very complexity of the system, built upon interwoven (and sometimes inconsistent) goals and aspirations, has made it ever more difficult to manage programs well and to make them responsive to the needs of citizens.

Discretion for the cities ⎯⎯⎯⎯⎯⎯⎯⎯⎯⎯⎯⎯⎯

By the end of the 1960s, most observers had concluded that federal urban aid programs had failed. In 1969 a presidential commission determined that the urban renewal program designed to help rebuild central cities had serious administrative problems and had "failed to help the poor." Model Cities, one of the most ambitious of all of Johnson's war-on-poverty programs, was according to one critic "the most unequivocal failure of all the 'Great Society' programs." The war on poverty had not been won, and many cities, in fact, seemed worse off than before the war began.[5]

Two issues were at the core of the problem. First, according to the U.S. General Accounting Office, administrative inefficiencies complicated the job of managing the programs well. Related programs were uncoordinated, and the great number of grant programs—nearly 450 in 1976—made coordination even more difficult. Local governments engaged in competitive grantsmanship for the available money. The application process was often plagued by confusion and red tape, and the processing of urban renewal applications took up to four years, an "unconscionable amount of time," according to a presidential commission.[6]

Second, critics complained that the growth of the system had created an imbalance between the federal and local governments. As the requirements became steadily more burdensome, local officials found they had less and less discretion over how to spend the money. Meanwhile, federal administrators who wrote the rules and local administrators who followed them came to dominate the process, a development that critics worried made the entire grant system more responsive to the narrow interests of a bureaucratic elite than to a broader public interest.

Nixon's response was to propose a "new federalism" that would change the foundation of intergovernmental aid. He argued that government had become too concentrated in Washington and that it was time "to start power and resources flowing back from Washington to the states and communities." The way to improve performance, he concluded, was to provide state and local governments "with more money and less interference." [7] This new federalism was to have two parts: general revenue sharing, a program of nearly unrestricted grants that Congress eagerly adopted in 1972; and special revenue sharing, a package of programs that stood between the narrow constraints of the earlier categorical grant programs and the more discretionary general revenue sharing. These special revenue-sharing programs were to give state and local elected officials, not administrators, principal control, and they were to grant money without competition or red tape. The key was local over federal choice, and decision making by elected generalists rather than administrative specialists.

The six special revenue-sharing programs, including programs for job training and community development, faced a much more difficult time in Congress. It was one thing to give money away through revenue sharing. It was quite another to declare a federal interest—for instance, in improving slums or training the unemployed—but to abandon federal control. Members of Congress worried about the ability of local officials to make good decisions and then to implement programs in a way that matched the often ambitious expectations of federal officials. Most members of the House favored simplifying the application process and removing as much red tape as possible. However, many members of the Senate—especially William Proxmire, D-Wis., of the key Senate Banking, Housing, and Urban Affairs Committee—did not completely trust local governments. Without strict federal control, some in Congress feared that the money would not be spent well and that the poor would suffer.

Worries about performance

After much debate, Congress finally passed the special revenue-sharing bill for community development, the Community Development Block Grant Program, in 1974. The program became a compromise between the more permissive House version and the more restrictive Senate version. The CD program consolidated into a single "block grant" seven of the Department of Housing and Urban Development's earlier grant programs, including the popular urban renewal and Model Cities programs. Cities with populations of more than 50,000 and counties with more than 200,000 automatically received an entitlement, determined by formula instead of by competition. Communities had to fill out applications describing what they intended to do with the money, but Congress's presumption was that the applications would be approved unless a community proposed something far out of keeping with the law's intent.

The CD program provided money for three general purposes: eliminating slums and blight, helping low- and moderate-income families, and meeting urgent community development needs. These categories covered an extremely broad menu of local activities, and local governments took advantage of the flexibility the CD program offered. Some communities' performance, however, demonstrated some of the worst fears members of Congress had expressed before the program's enactment.

Conflicts in Bridgeport

One such community was Bridgeport, Connecticut, an industrial town that was gradually losing its industry to other cities and its wealthy citizens to prosperous suburbs.[8] As a result, the central business district was deteriorating and the town was becoming a less pleasant place to live. With $405,000 of the $4.1 million that the city received from the CD program, city officials decided to improve neighborhood parks. Although Bridgeport's nickname was "The Park City," many neighborhoods had little open space left.

When planners requested the money for parks, however, they had not yet figured out what the money would buy. Combing their files for earlier proposals, they found two projects that had been stalled by the lack of local funds. Park department officials earmarked $113,000 of the $405,000 for building tennis courts in the city's relatively affluent North End and reclaiming a dumping ground under an elevated section of the Connecticut Turnpike in the lower income South End.

Park planners suggested spending the remaining $300,000 on four more parks: a neighborhood playground for the relatively poor East End; a park in the central business district; a softball field in the affluent North End; and a park along the city's waterfront. Almost immediately, however, the projects hit a snag. The city's charter required the park board to approve all park projects, and some members of the board spoke against the East End playground, the one project of the four directed toward the city's poor. The planners prevented opponents from picking the plan apart by packaging all of the plans together into a single project and finally won approval. Then they began an environmental review, required of all projects funded with federal money, to determine if any of the projects would harm the environment.

Each of these steps compounded the delay of the projects: deciding how to spend the money, winning approval from the park board, and preparing the environmental impact statement. Halfway through the program's first year in 1975, Bridgeport had spent no money at all on these park projects. When finally the city began the softball field in the North End in early 1976, neighborhood residents surprised park planners with their outrage. They bitterly complained that the softball field would bring noise, congestion, and "undesirables" into their neighborhood. One city staff member was more blunt. "They are afraid of minority people coming into their neighborhood," he explained. Project officials believed that neighborhood residents preferred no new park at all if blacks and Hispanics might use the new softball field.

Park department officials decided they ought to hold public hearings before moving any further. These hearings established beyond doubt that the residents wanted no park near their homes, so the planners suggested instead that the city build two new tennis courts in an existing park far away from the homes. City residents complained even more strongly that tennis courts in the town's most affluent neighborhood would not help the low- and moderate-income people to whom Congress, at least in part, had directed the CD program. The park board dismissed the complaints and, at long last, began work.

When the city received its next $4.1 million entitlement in 1976, the citizens' task force decided to avoid the previous year's problems. Instead of concentrating the money in certain neighborhoods, the task force recommended spending $730,600 to put parks in *all* of Bridgeport's neighborhoods, with nineteen to be built. That decision avoided all of the problems of the previous year. Every member of the task force could return to his or her neighborhood with a new park; as one city staff member explained, it was a way to "give everybody a piece of something."

Mayor John Mandanici and the city council later trimmed the park plan back to $300,000, because the mayor wanted to use some of the money for housing rehabilitation and a juvenile delinquency program. Predictably, instead of eliminating some proposed parks from the plan, the city decided to fund *all* of the parks at a reduced scale. Everyone, in the end, got his park. Even so it took almost the entire year to begin even the scaled-back projects.

The city ran into even deeper problems with an ambitious project to improve its downtown waterfront. The Pequonnock River had once been scenic, but by the early 1970s abandoned factories, petroleum tank farms, and junkyards cluttered the river banks. The first sight greeting visitors to the city was the deteriorating waterfront, and for Bridgeport residents the waterfront placed a stigma on the downtown. City officials had tried before to clean up the area. An $8 million project called

Congress Plaza was to have brought new housing and commerce downtown, but the project created little more than vacant land and boarded-up buildings. One disgruntled resident in the late 1970s hung a sign on a closed movie theater that read: "You are looking at the center of Congress Plaza. Hopes have grown from promises made by City Hall in 1971. Is this the spirit in which City Hall keeps all of its promises? Don't hold your breath to find out—this building is still waiting."

But city officials were more hopeful about the new project. Private developers had brought jai alai to one vacant tract along the Pequonnock, and city planners suggested that CD money could be used to develop the opposite bank. The citizens' task force agreed that something ought to be done with the area and recommended that the city spend $100,000 on some unspecified project. When John Mandanici took office in January 1976, he decided that the waterfront park project would become the center of his CD program for Bridgeport, but his plans were no more concrete.

City planners returned with an ambitious agenda for building a marina, a new pier for walking and fishing, a bikeway, and attractive benches and lighting to encourage people to enjoy the river. These projects, they hoped, would complement the jai alai facility across the river and would anchor an even more ambitious redevelopment of the waterfront, including rehabilitation of the city's old railroad station and transformation of an old Staten Island ferryboat from New York into a scenic restaurant.

While the mayor liked the plans, the citizens' task force—part of the city's citizen participation required by the CD law—did not. Some members suggested that the project was more properly a job for private enterprise. Even more significant to the task force was that city planners had announced the project without consulting the citizens' group. They were enraged that, in the words of some members, city officials were engaging in "underhandedness" and trying to "push the project down our throats." They were also angry that, while one of their favorite projects—a neighborhood center for the poor East End—moved along slowly, city planners were moving very quickly on the waterfront project.

The task force decided to complain directly to HUD by arguing that the waterfront project was not an eligible project under HUD's rules for the CD program. HUD agreed with the task force, ruling that the marina *was* ineligible because it was, in essence, a transit terminal. (Transit terminals could not be built with CD funds.) By the time HUD acted, however, city officials had already halted planning for the marina. In charting the area they discovered underwater two sunken barges of the type that once navigated the famous Erie Canal. The State Historic Preservation Commission determined that the barges had great historical value and ordered the city not to destroy them. Raising the barges intact would cost $105,000—more than the $100,000 the city allocated to the project in the first year and one-fifth of the $510,000 the city had budgeted for the entire project. (Of this amount, $100,000 was to come from the CD program's second year fund, another $130,000 from the third year, and a $280,000 matching grant from the federal Bureau of Outdoor Recreation.) Every alternative explored seemed to promise more delays, so the city decided to drop the marina from the project just as it received word from HUD that it was ineligible anyway.

No sooner had planners developed a revised, less ambitious proposal than another problem arose. City officials discovered that they did not own the land on which they proposed to build the park, and the Bureau of Outdoor Recreation funded projects only on publicly owned land. The Consolidated Rail Corporation owned some of the land and leased it to the state Department of Transportation for its commuter rail service, which subleased it to the city. A local privately owned electric company owned another parcel. The city then started a long series of negotiations to obtain rights to the land. By early 1977 city officials finally had acquired all the land they needed, and they announced that they were ready to start.

New delays surfaced, however. Bridgeport officials learned they needed a permit from the state Department of Environmental Protection because the Pequonnock River was an inland waterway. Because it was a navigable river, the city also needed several permits from the U.S. Army Corps of Engineers. Finally, late in the spring of 1977, the city collected all of the permits and began removing pilings from the river. However, Bridgeport still had not received word on its application for the federal matching grant from the Bureau of Outdoor Recreation, and the project was dormant, awaiting a decision. More than two years after planning began, the Waterfront Park was still no more than a plan, but in subsequent years the park did take shape—but not in the way city officials had hoped.

Bridgeport's painful experiences with the CD program brought to life many of the worries that members of Congress had about leaving more decisions to local officials. The parks projects were little more than ill-disguised patronage, with parks distributed to each of the city's neighborhoods. The projects illustrated a fundamental truth about the CD program: left on their own, local politicians faced irresistible pressures to sprinkle the money broadly around communities instead of planning where it might do the most good. On the other hand, the waterfront project demonstrated the dangers that befell projects when local officials' ambitions exceeded their administrative capacity. Bridgeport officials simply could not marshal the resources required to begin work on the project, for at every turn they discovered new roadblocks.

Federal reactions

Not all cities suffered from such problems. Many had great success in using federal money for housing rehabilitation, recreation programs, and downtown renovations, among many other projects. But the uneven record of local governments—both in making decisions and in administering projects—led to great restiveness on Capitol Hill and in HUD.

Who decides?

Local flexibility had always been the keystone of the community development program, but critics of the program were concerned that without federal control the money would not reach the poor. Many interest groups had pressed for guidelines in the CD legislation that would force communities to earmark a substantial part of their grants for the most needy. While the Senate had concentrated on directing money to the poor, members of the House had focused most on relieving the red tape connected with earlier programs. The final act was, not surprisingly, a compromise. Communities were to spend their money on projects giving "maximum feasible priority to activities which will benefit low- and moderate-income families [from the Senate version of the bill] or aid in the prevention or elimination of slums and blight" or meet urgent community development needs (from the House version).[9] Local governments simply had to certify that their local projects met one of these objectives.

Local governments soon proved more imaginative than HUD officials or members of Congress ever expected. Waste disposal facilities were eligible—but what about animal crematoriums? Senior citizens' programs were eligible—but what about citizens' band radios for senior citizens' buses? In one case, HUD ruled that CD funds could help build a garden but could not buy the tools or the seeds to be used in it. To make matters worse, interpretations of the eligibility of projects varied wildly across the country, and clever local officials shopped around for interpretations that favored projects they wanted to build.

The CD program's flexibility, combined with HUD's confusion about which projects were eligible, gave local officials great maneuvering room in deciding what to do. The Southern Regional Council's monitoring project suggested that the poor were suffering much more under CD than under previous federally controlled programs that forced communities to focus on the needy. In fact, a coalition of interest groups, calling itself the Working Group for Community Development Reform, charged that "funds have too frequently been diverted from low and moderate income persons who need them most, particularly in the wealthier and suburban areas." [10] Two careful studies in 1975 and 1976 provided more evidence: apparently only about 50 to 55 percent of CD funds was finding its way to the poor. [11] "All of the monitoring studies of the program," a staff study for the House Subcommittee on Housing and Community Development said, "conclude that the low- and moderate-income objectives of the act are not being met." [12]

Much of this evidence came before congressional hearings, and Senator Proxmire blasted HUD for "about as powerful an indictment of an administrative agency that I have ever heard." HUD had gotten the program underway, he said, but "What isn't clear is whether the program you have been administering is the program Congress passed." [13] Faced with such congressional pressure, HUD in the Ford administration gradually began tightening up the rules to focus more money on the poor.

Republicans in the mid-1970s had aimed to loosen the strings on federal aid—in part to reduce the federal government's power. In part, some critics suggested, they had also wanted to outflank liberal members of the bureaucracy who had become entrenched since Lyndon Johnson's Great Society. When the Democrats returned to power with the Carter administration, they were determined to focus federal attention on the issue of who was benefiting from the programs. Patricia Roberts Harris, Jimmy Carter's HUD secretary, tried to tighten the rules still further. She stressed the importance of concentrating benefits on low- and moderate-income persons and promised that HUD would review local applications more carefully. In response to the continuing stream of complaints from interest groups and some members of Congress, HUD also proposed regulations that would have forced communities to allocate at least 75 percent of their money to the poor. But other members of Congress strongly objected, reminding HUD that one of the program's principal goals was to loosen federal strings on urban aid. HUD withdrew the rules but promised to keep a 75 percent target for aid to the poor. Communities that could not show that three-fourths of their CD money went "principally for persons of low- and moderate-income" courted much closer HUD inspection of their activities. HUD also encouraged communities to designate "neighborhood strategy areas," more needy neighborhoods in which local governments promised to concentrate development money. In return, local officials could use the other 25 percent of their funds for politically popular projects like the recreation programs Bridgeport proposed in relatively more affluent neighborhoods.

Bridgeport's experience, in fact, demonstrated the CD program's dilemma. The federal programs of the 1960s had undoubtedly become so enmeshed in applications requirements and restrictions on the use of the funds that effective management was extremely difficult. Furthermore, many critics believed that the domination of programs by appointed administrators at all levels made accountability harder to ensure. Loosening the federal strings and putting more power in the hands of local elected officials thus made great sense. On the other hand, these local officials faced the same political pressures as elected officials everywhere. It is always very difficult to concentrate money narrowly on any group—even the poor—and to exclude consciously other groups—and voters. Congress dealt with this by enacting a formula that guaranteed a very broad distribution of CD money, including funds to some relatively well-to-do communities. In the communities, local elected officials not surprisingly often spread projects around broadly, like the parks in Bridgeport, to build political support. When the opposite complaints grew—that the poor were being shortchanged by a program whose key objective was aid to the poor—HUD's administrators began tightening the reins.

The dilemma was a clear one. Relying on local officials diminished the problems of federal red tape but also often meant distributing the money more widely. On the other hand, ensuring that the money was concentrated more narrowly—on blighted neighborhoods or needy people—meant much tighter federal administrative controls and more requirements. The decision about who was to decide made the trade-offs even clearer.

What is success?

Critics also worried about the mixed performance of local governments in the CD program. Some communities ran extremely successful projects, for instance, a housing rehabilitation program in New Haven, Connecticut, that renewed more than 300 homes. Just up the coast, the city of New London renovated its downtown with a plan remarkably similar to the one that foundered in Bridgeport. New London rebuilt a half-dozen buildings, helped rehabilitate the city's old railroad station to include a new restaurant, developed a new pier, and attracted a major festival of sailing ships.[14] Such projects were palpable triumphs: citizens could sense the transformation of their towns and, in some cases, a remarkable change in civic spirit.

Other communities had far less success in managing their projects. Despite its great plans, Bridgeport in the CD program's first years did little but raise hopes—then dash them. Meanwhile, in Norwich, Connecticut, an ambitious project to build a new tower housing the elderly, complete with ground-floor shops, failed when local opposition began to grow. The city backtracked and instead constructed a parking garage. Another project to rehabilitate some old mill houses hit snag after snag that delayed all work for more than three years as the city's novice CD staff struggled with the requisite plans and approvals.[15] A combination of local political conflict, ambitious plans, and an inability to muster enough administrative expertise to solve problems produced lengthy delays and, sometimes, outright failures.

Indeed, "success" is hard to measure when such a wide range of organizations is involved. At the federal level, some members of Congress viewed success as targeting money on the poor, while others saw success in less federal involvement. At the local level, success often lay in the decision to distribute the money, while other officials focused more on the end result. Success in fact emerged as a highly relative term, its definition depending on one's perspective. That, in fact, may be the central truth of government by proxy as exercised through federal grants. The often disparate goals of federal, state, and local governments—their elected officials, administrators, citizens, and interest groups—means that judging success has always been a difficult business. "Success" can only be measured against a goal, and each member of this intricate partnership has a different vision about what ought to be accomplished.

One person's success was sometimes another's failure. In Norwich, for example, even though most officials favored the senior citizens' housing project, one member of the city council campaigned against it. He rallied enough opposition to stop it—a huge success from his point of view, but a major disappointment from the perspective of city planners. Sometimes success was a gradual process. In New Haven, a major effort to rebuild decaying downtown buildings had mixed results. It took a long time for the restored buildings and theaters to emerge, and they turned out to be different from what city officials had originally planned. The more ambitious the plan, the more complicated was its administration and the more likely it was to encounter problems, delays, political conflict, and evolutionary change. Thus, while everyone wanted success, just what constituted success was not always apparent or universally accepted. The program's goals were so broad that an extraordinary range of projects was eligible. As one official at the U.S. Office of Management and Budget noted, "It's hard to get good information on a program like CD when you don't know what it's supposed to do." [16]

Finding out what was actually happening with federal money was also difficult. A group of college students monitoring CD projects as part of an internship program was sent out one day to check up on a local recreation program. They visited a recreation center where youngsters were supposed to be getting a photography lesson. When they arrived, they were told that the children had gone bowling instead. The students then went to the bowling alley and were told the youngsters had already left. The monitors worried that perhaps nothing was going on at all. [17]

HUD, in fact, put more emphasis on distributing the money and supervising the flow of paper than in overseeing the program's results. Monitoring usually meant checking the file cabinets to make sure that the proper forms had been filed. [18] HUD instead relied principally on communities' own reports on their progress—reports the U.S. General Accounting Office found were often vague at best and at worst suspect. One community reported an activity as "parking lots" and listed the benefit as to "provide parking facilities." As for progress, the community said that the "central lot [was] acquired" and the "parking structure [was] underway." Such reports were not precise enough to keep HUD well-informed about its programs. [19]

As a result, HUD had little information on performance. When asked how much the agency knew about local activities, one HUD staffer replied, "Very little. Headquarters is so removed from reality. The opportunities for gathering information are limited, and we consequently spend much of our time shuffling paper. As a result, the monitoring complaints and the newspaper articles take on exaggerated importance because we don't have other sources of information. We knee-jerk a lot to unbalance criticism because we have such a small staff and relatively few opportunities to get information." [20]

The elusive search for accountability _____

In pursuing domestic policy through federal grants, policy makers are thus caught in a dilemma. Federal grants fundamentally exist to serve some national purpose, as shaped by a complex policy-making system composed of the legislative branch, the executive branch, courts, program administrators and staff members, and interest groups. That purpose, the result of diverse pressures, typically is stated in extremely vague compromise language, the meaning of which evolves after a bill is passed. State and local governments, on the other hand, naturally want the flexibility to use federal money to seek their own goals, goals often different from the federal government's and just as fuzzy. State and local administrative capacity, moreover, often varies greatly, as does the success of subnational governments in carrying out the projects they attempt.

Federal grants therefore have gone through cycles of centralization and decentralization, of strengthened federal control giving way to demands for restoring discretion to state and local governments. On the other hand, state and local governments, when given more discretion, inevitably make some decisions that do not match what some policy makers at the federal level would prefer. The result quite naturally is renewed pressure for recentralization. Indeed, centralization and decentralization are not alternatives but, rather, two poles between which federal-state-local relations continually swing.[21]

With each swing, though, there is a tendency for the intergovernmental system to become even more encrusted with regulations to govern the way state and local officials spend their money. Each movement toward decentralization often retains the rules from earlier centralizations, rules ranging from civil rights to environmental protection. These rules add costs to local operations. In Newark, New Jersey, for example, meeting the standards of the 1977 Clean Air Act required a $51.8 million capital investment and another $10.4 million in annual operating expenses.[22] The rules, furthermore, are often inconsistently administered, not only on what to do but on how to do it. The U.S. Advisory Commission on Intergovernmental Relations, in noting the "regulatory proclivities" of Congress and the executive branch, argued, "Intergovernmental conflict and confusion have hampered progress toward achieving national goals."[23]

Despite the fundamental American reverence for local control, the basic reflex in response to problems in programs often is to add layers of federal guidelines. The result is often an intergovernmental system in conflict between federal control and state-local discretion. From the federal perspective, the difficulty of reconciling federal, state, and local goals hinders administrative performance and muddies accountability. Federal program managers find it frustrating to try to guide programs ultimately administered by state and local officials in thousands of governments. From the state and local perspective, the challenge is to meet widely varying local needs within the restrictions imposed by program-based and across-the-board regulation. In short, federal grants have all of the typical problems of government by proxy complicated by a constitutional system that retains substantial autonomy for the states.

Reconciling goals: the Connecticut NIS _____

Complicating these problems still further in the early 1980s were the budget cuts of Reagan's "new federalism." Reagan, committed to increasing defense spending and reducing the federal government's domestic role, had a specific intergovernmental agenda: fewer federal regulations in return for less money. After several battles in Congress, Reagan won a substantial part of his program, and federal aid to state and local government dropped $6.6 billion, a cut of 12 percent, allowing for inflation.

This new federalism passed along to the states some extremely difficult problems, especially that of meeting growing demands for services as the money dried up. In Connecticut, for example, one of the Reagan administration's new block grants for social services cut spending by nearly one-third and left to the state the responsibility for deciding how to spend the money. The potential political problems were enormous. The state had much less money to spend on its growing social service needs—day care, legal services, counseling, and home health care.

Officials in Connecticut's Office of Policy and Management decided to try a new strategy for dealing with the cuts. Rather than starting a battle with a host of service agencies struggling over a smaller pot of money, the officials convinced Democratic governor William O'Neill to try an approach developed by the Charles F. Kettering Foundation. Out of concern that many federal programs to aid the cities were uncoordinated and contentious, the foundation had conducted pilot projects (in St. Paul, Minnesota; Columbus, Ohio; and Gary, Indiana) demonstrating that a "negotiated investment strategy" could improve local decisions. The NIS, as it was known, brought together local officials, federal administrators, and representatives of local groups that would receive the money. Together they hammered out a budget that nearly everyone agreed was successful: the level of disagreement was lower, and the projects funded were better coodinated than would otherwise have been the case.[24]

With the help of the Kettering Foundation, Connecticut's Office of Policy and Management launched a short-term effort to negotiate the cuts and reduce the inevitable conflicts. The office formed a negotiating team from the three principal groups. One group was the collection of fourteen state agencies that would administer or receive funding from the new social services block grant. A second group was the nearly one thousand nonprofit organizations most affected by the grant, organizations that together administered about two-thirds of Connecticut's grant. (The program was a proxy-on-proxy strategy: the federal government relied on the state government to run the program. Most of the state's money, in turn, was administered by its own grantees and contractors.) A final group was the array of local governments affected by the decisions. Each group had five representatives, and mediators joined the fifteen negotiators to help them reach agreement.

It was a high-stakes strategy. The budget cuts had raised the level of conflict, and the participants had such different perspectives that agreement would not be easy. Furthermore, the process outflanked the state's usual decision-making apparatus, for instance, the state legislature. Still, state officials feared that business as usual might increase the political conflict even more—as everyone competed for slices of a smaller pie. And the old methods might prove inefficient as political horsetrading rather than service needs determined the outcome.

The negotiators debated competing positions in highly structured meetings. They tried first to agree on which problems were the most serious and therefore ought to be the focus of the most money. That process produced a surprising degree of agreement, although the negotiators won a consensus in part because they passed some of the difficult issues on to the second stage, the allocation of the money. The allocation stage was much more contentious, but in the end, the negotiators conceived a plan for spending the money.

The negotiators spent most of their time setting priorities in formal documents that they then signed. The team asked whether they should serve the physically or sexually abused by providing intervention or shelter. Should they provide aid in emergency situations? Should they aim at alleviating the need for more expensive services in the future? They then decided on high-priority services (such as child care and emergency shelter), medium-priority services (family planning and foster care), and low-priority services (counseling and recreation). This ranking provided the basis for budgeting the money.

The participants generally were happy with the results. All but two of the fifteen participants, in fact, said that the process had exceeded their expectations. They also agreed that the results were fairer than the usual process of bargaining would have produced and that the decisions better matched the state's needs. In a very short time, they produced agreement on an exceptionally complex problem and, in the process, improved communication among all of the participants. The process, moreover, was more open, with broader representation of the various groups than would otherwise have been the case. One participant admitted that the team did not really define "the major issues in human services, but it did establish a process whereby communication among the three sectors now sets the stage for open and comprehensive planning and coordinating among human services agencies."

It was an expensive process. The negotiating sessions cost thousands of dollars in support from the Kettering Foundation, and other foundations contributed more money to pay for the mediators. Expenditures totaled more than $76,000. In addition, the process took a great deal of time. Each negotiator spent about ten days in group meetings, plus about two or three times that amount in smaller sessions. Virtually every participant believed that the process took more time than previous budgeting sessions, but nearly everyone believed that the improved results made the time and expense worthwhile.

Grants, values, and goals

A negotiated investment strategy, of course, does not fit every intergovernmental problem. Connecticut's experiment was a short-term attempt to solve difficult problems. It worked because the cuts were so drastic that everyone realized the potential problems were enormous and because the governor and his staff were committed to making the NIS work. The state and the foundations, furthermore, were willing to spend the resources—money and staff time—that the process required. When problems are more routine, when the expectations are too great, or when the resources are too small, a negotiated approach would probably not work nearly so well. Still, the NIS approach is a real opportunity for lowering conflict and improving intergovernmental decisions while striving for agreement on goals.

Even more important, both the problems of the CD program and the success of the NIS demonstrate that intergovernmental politics revolves around questions of values and goals. Different participants at different levels of the federal system typically have different goals, and these differences predictably generate conflict. In the CD program, the Washington-based interest groups wanted the money concentrated on the poor; HUD vacillated between seeking narrow targeting and procedural flexibility; and, at the local level, a diverse set of interests struggled to define how best to meet local needs, both political and economic.

Government by proxy, at its core, means operating governmental programs through different organizations, each with different goals. The Connecticut NIS experiment demonstrates that these conflicts can be reduced, but only by developing a process for reconciling the widely different values that are the very essence of America's intergovernmental system. Administrative problems of securing good performance always remain, but the fundamental battles are waged over conflicts of values—different visions for the conduct of American federalism and, more broadly, of American government.

Notes

1. Raymond Brown, Ann Coil, and Carol Rose, *A Time for Accounting* (Atlanta: Southern Regional Council, 1976), 53, 59, 60-61, 102; U.S. Congress, Senate, Committee on Banking, Housing, and Urban Affairs, *Community Development Block Grant Program*, hearings, 94th Cong., 2d sess., 1976, 25.
2. Jane Perry Clark Carey, *The Rise of a New Federalism* (New York: Columbia University Press, 1938).
3. U.S. Office of Management and Budget, *Budget of the United States Government, Fiscal Year 1987, Special Analyses* (Washington, D.C.: U.S. Government Printing Office, 1986), H19.
4. U.S. Advisory Commission on Intergovernmental Relations, *Regulatory Federalism* (Washington, D.C.: U.S. Government Printing Office, 1984), 7-11.
5. U.S. National Commission on Urban Problems, *Building the American City* (Washington, D.C.: U.S. Government Printing Office, 1968), 165-167; Christopher C. DeMuth, "Deregulating the Cities," *The Public Interest*, no. 44 (1976): 115.
6. U.S. Comptroller General, *Fundamental Changes Are Needed in Federal Assistance to State and Local Governments* (Washington, D.C.: U.S. General Accounting Office, 1975), GGD-75-75, 9; National Commission, *Building the American City*, 165.
7. U.S. Office of the Federal Register, *Weekly Compilation of Presidential Documents* 7 (January 25, 1971), 92, 93.
8. The case comes from Donald F. Kettl, *Managing Community Development in the New Federalism* (New York: Praeger Publishers, 1980), 64-73.
9. Public Law 93-383, Sec. 104(b)(2).
10. See the testimony of Peter Buschbaum for the Working Group for Community Development Reform, U.S. Congress, Senate, Committee on Banking, Housing, and Urban Affairs, *Housing and Community Development Legislation of 1977*, hearings, 95th Cong., 1st sess., 1977, 443-444.
11. Robert L. Ginsberg, "Second Year Community Development Block Grant Experience: A Summary of the Findings of the NAHRO Community Development Monitoring Project (January 1977)," *Journal of Housing* 34 (February 1977): 80-83; Richard P. Nathan and Associates, *Block Grants for Community Development* (Washington, D.C.: Brookings, 1977), 308.

12. U.S. Congress, House of Representatives, Committee on Banking, Finance, and Urban Affairs, *Community Development Block Grant Program*, committee print, 95th Cong., 1st sess., 1977, 21.
13. Senate Banking Committee, *CD Program*, 380, 505, 533.
14. See Kettl, *Managing Community Development*, 41-44, 53-57.
15. Ibid., 73-83.
16. Donald F. Kettl, *The Regulation of American Federalism* (Baton Rouge: Louisiana State University Press, 1983), 81.
17. Interviews with the author.
18. Kettl, *The Regulation of American Federalism*, 81.
19. U.S. Comptroller General, *Management and Evaluation of the Community Development Block Grant Program Need to Be Strengthened* (Washington, D.C.: U.S. General Accounting Office, 1978), Report CED-78-160, 3-4.
20. Quoted in Kettl, *The Regulation of American Federalism*, 78.
21. See James W. Fesler, "Approaches to the Understanding of Decentralization," *Journal of Politics* 27 (August 1965): 536-566; Herbert Kaufman, "Emerging Conflicts in the Doctrines of Public Administration," *American Political Science Review* 50 (December 1956): 1057-1073.
22. Advisory Commission, *Regulatory Federalism*, 12.
23. Ibid, 246.
24. Case comes from Armentrout and Associates, *Evaluation of the Connecticut Negotiated Investment Strategy Experiment* (Atlanta: photocopied, 1983).

Tax expenditures: the struggle over tax reform 4

Tax reform was the keystone of Ronald Reagan's domestic policy for his second administration. Walter Mondale's 1984 presidential campaign had wrecked on the rocks of a proposed tax increase and Reagan was even more determined after the election to avoid raising taxes. Reagan argued in a May 1985 speech to the nation that federal income taxes needed real reform "to transform a system that's become an endless source of confusion and resentment into one that is clear, simple, and fair for all." For too long, he said, the tax system had encouraged individuals and corporations to put their money in certain investments purely for tax purposes, a practice that unfairly helped some avoid taxes altogether while most Americans had to carry the burden. He promised nothing less than "a second American revolution," one "born of popular resentment against a tax system that is unwise, unwanted, and unfair." With his plan for tax reform, he promised, "the free rides are over." [1]

Even though taxes were a central issue in the 1984 presidential campaign, it was a Washington public-interest lobbyist who perhaps played the strongest role in galvanizing the political system for change. Robert S. McIntyre, of the Citizens for Tax Justice, had campaigned since 1981 against "loophole lobbyists" and the unfairness of the income tax system. He examined publicly available corporate reports from 250 of the largest American companies, and he found that more than half—130 companies—paid no income taxes in at least one year from 1981 to 1985. Over the same period, 42 companies paid no overall taxes and, in fact, received more than $2 billion in rebates from the federal government, even though they earned $56.8 billion in pretax domestic profits.[2]

McIntyre also released a list of what he called "the top ten corporate freeloaders," led by AT&T, which from 1982 to 1985 earned profits of nearly $25 billion yet received federal income tax rebates of $635 million. Overall, his top ten earned $39.7 billion but received federal tax rebates of $1.5 billion. Even though the official corporate income tax rate was 46 percent, the average tax rate of these companies was *minus* 3.8 percent: they received, on the average, nearly $4 back from the federal government for every $100 of profits. McIntyre's message was a simple one: the constant changes in the tax code, designed to further a broad range of objectives, had instead created an unfair tax system.[3]

Newspaper stories based on McIntyre's findings enraged many taxpayers, and many members of Congress as well. The resulting furor gave a powerful push to Reagan's tax reform proposal. After eighteen months of struggle, and several emergency resuscitations, a tax reform bill finally passed, although in a form very different from Reagan's original proposal. Nevertheless, the president proudly proclaimed it one of his biggest accomplishments. "This tax bill is less a reform," he said on signing it, "than a revolution." And he quipped as the New York Mets were beating the Boston Red Sox in the 1986 World Series, "I feel like we just played the World Series of tax reform and the American people won."[4]

The tax code and social policy

Tax reform has been on the agenda of nearly every presidency since Congress first passed the federal income tax in 1913. From those first years, tax rates and deductions from income have been the issues in a constant battle. The tax rate battle has raged over whether the rich should pay more taxes than the poor, a system economists call "progressivity." Federal individual income tax rates have always been progressive: as individuals make more money, they move into higher income tax brackets, and as the brackets rise taxpayers have had to pay a higher percentage of their income. In 1913 the top rate was 7 percent, far less than the 70 percent rate the wealthiest taxpayers paid in 1980 on income in the highest bracket. The 1981 tax act reduced the top rate to 50 percent, and—as we shall see—the 1986 tax reform bill reduced it even further.[5]

The issue of deductions has been even more complex. The tax code has never treated all income and expenditures equally. Instead, the tax laws have been designed to encourage individuals and corporations to spend their money and earn income in ways Congress and the president deemed socially desirable. These special preferences have been called by a variety of names: "tax expenditures," by economic experts who suggest that not collecting tax revenue because of these preferences is the same as spending it directly; "tax breaks," by most people who look on them as special advantages in the tax code that help them reduce their taxes; and "tax loopholes," by all of us when we talk about the tax breaks that *others* use to reduce their taxes in ways we think are unfair.

We will use the term *tax expenditures*, which emphasizes the important point that these programs are in many ways interchangeable with federal spending programs. Tax expenditures have the same effect on the deficit, and they can achieve many of the same purposes as federal programs. At their core, they create incentives for individuals and corporations to behave in ways that are intended, more or less, to further goals defined in the tax laws. However, tax expenditures in practice are not identical with related spending programs. They can have very different effects on economic growth and can affect people in different income groups very differently. These issues, in fact, underlie much of the debate on tax expenditures.

Kinds of tax expenditures

Tax expenditures are of three kinds. First, there are *tax deductions*, which allow individuals and corporations to deduct certain expenses from their income. The individuals and corporations thus escape paying taxes on money used for these expenses, and their tax bills are lower than they would otherwise be. From the beginning, the tax code has allowed corporations to deduct basic expenses of doing business, such as the costs of state and local taxes and of interest on business loans. Similarly, individuals have long been allowed to deduct state and local taxes (such as individual income taxes), interest paid on borrowed money (such as home mortgages), and charitable contributions. The purpose of these deductions is simple, but the public goals are varied and complex. For example, one aim is to make home ownership more affordable by reducing the real cost of the mortgage and taxes; another is to encourage taxpayers to support charitable organizations by allowing tax-deductible contributions to nonprofit groups.

The federal government encourages other goals through a second strategy, *tax exclusions*. Some income is not subject to income taxation at all—for instance, interest earned on municipal bonds, a shorthand term for state and local bonds. Ever since the federal income tax began, the tax code has encouraged investors to support such borrowing. Because interest earned on these bonds is not subject to federal (and, in some cases, state and local) taxation, taxpayers get to keep the interest instead of surrendering it to the government in taxes. The higher the individual's tax bracket, the more attractive this exclusion is. Yet, because the exclusion makes these municipal bonds more attractive, state and local governments do not have to pay as high a rate of interest on the bonds as they otherwise might, so their borrowing cost is less. Taxpayers as well as state and local governments end up ahead; it is the federal treasury that suffers.

Finally, the federal government gives *tax credits* for some expenditures. These credits are more valuable than deductions or exclusions because they count against the taxes owed instead of income earned. For example, the federal government long allowed individuals and corporations a 10 percent credit for investments made to improve their businesses. If an automobile manufacturer bought a new piece of machinery for the assembly line, the company could reduce its tax bill by 10 percent of the cost. During the energy crisis, the federal government wanted to encourage homeowners to improve the energy efficiency of their homes. Money spent to insulate an attic or install storm windows could be directly subtracted from the tax bill. Thus, a $100 investment in insulation reduced taxes by $100. The same investment, if allowed as a deduction, would have reduced taxes by only $33 for a typical upper-middle-class family in the 33 percent tax bracket.

Tax expenditures as incentives

No matter what their form, all of these tax expenditures had a central purpose: to create incentives for individuals and corporations to act according to purposes defined in the tax code and perhaps differently from the way they might otherwise have behaved. For example, more individuals buy homes, and they purchase larger homes than they would have had the deduction not lowered the cost.

Tax expenditures are notoriously difficult to measure. According to Congress's Joint Committee on Taxation, they totaled $424.5 billion in fiscal 1986, with $119.9 billion going to corporations and $304.6 billion to individuals.[6] However, these totals are higher than the amount of revenue the government would have received had all the tax expenditures been repealed. Each tax expenditure is intended to change individual and corporate behavior, and it is hard to estimate precisely what taxpayers' behavior (and, therefore, tax revenue) would have been without them. Without question, however, even after the major tax reform legislation of 1986, tax expenditures amount to a sizable loss of federal revenue. Tax expenditures still dwarf the size of the federal deficit and rank among the largest of the federal government's programs, along with social security, the defense budget, and federal loans.

Tax expenditures cost the federal government money, and complying with the federal and state income tax imposes substantial costs on taxpayers. In 1982 the cost of completing federal and state tax forms was, according to economists' estimates, between $17 billion and $27 billion—5 to 7 percent of all the money raised by the income tax system. Taxpayers spent 2 billion hours filling out tax returns and paid $3 billion to professional tax preparers.[7]

As the tax code became more complicated over the years, some individuals and corporations skillfully found ways to exploit its intricacies. In the mid-1980s, for example, even though the top income tax rate was 50 percent, no corporate income group paid more than 26 percent of its income on the average. The corporations on Robert McIntyre's "top ten" list got there by exploiting provisions in the corporate tax code. After the 1981 tax law, corporations paid on the average only about 13 percent of their income in taxes, despite the 46 percent tax rate.[8]

So complicated did the tax system become that taxpayers were losing confidence in it. A public opinion poll revealed that 23 percent of Americans admitted underreporting their income or overstating their deductions, and more than half of all those surveyed believed that cheating was frequent.[9] Syndicated columnist James J. Kilpatrick sharply criticized "sleazy schemes of tax avoidance" whose object "is not to earn money but to lose money—to provide tax losses for the rich." Kilpatrick and many other critics feared that the result would be a diversion of capital from productive investments to investments whose sole value was their tax impact. The nation's long-run economic health, as well as short-run confidence in the tax system, he warned, was likely to suffer.[10]

While everyone agreed that the tax system was unfair, changing it seemed to be politically a no-win situation. Any tax system was bound to be more painful to some persons and companies than to others, and the existing system had its own supporters—those who benefited from its provisions. Any change rearranging tax expenditures would undoubtedly stir enormous opposition from those losing their tax breaks. Meanwhile, the political constituency for a fairer tax system was fuzzy. Support for "fairness" could never create the same strong emotions as opposition to lost deductions. Members of Congress could not specify exactly how much a fairer tax system would help or hurt their districts overall, but every member—through the mailbag—was acutely aware of the individuals and corporations who believed that a change might severely hurt them. The lesson was clear. Political support for tax reform was likely to be broad but diffuse; opposition, on the other hand, was certain to be sharp and pointed. It was a political game in which winning was hard but losing was very easy.

Rocky road to reform

For more than twenty years before the monumental tax reform act of 1986, the federal tax system had ridden a roller coaster of change. Congress enacted major cuts in 1964 followed by large tax increases in 1969. During the 1970s, the nation's weak economy prompted recurring changes, all designed to revive the economy but each in a different way. Even more important, each change made the tax code more complex and more tailored to promote certain kinds of investment or to protect certain kinds of income. In 1926 the tax code was only 136 pages long. Fifty years later in 1976, the index alone was 125 pages. Form 1040 used to report income was 2 pages long in 1926 but had grown to 13 pages fifty years later.[11]

By the late 1970s both the public and the politicians were becoming distressed about the complexity and disincentives of the tax code. President Jimmy Carter called the income tax system a disgrace to the human race and in speeches complained about the "three-martini lunch," the expensive meals business executives deducted on their income tax returns. Carter pointed to a classic case of a businessman who deducted 338 lunches in one year, for which he spent more than $10,000. (That amounted to a business lunch almost every day of the year, with each lunch averaging nearly $30.)[12] Carter's attempt to reform the tax code fell short because of congressional opposition, but three years later Congress proved to be much more receptive to Ronald Reagan's plan.

In 1981 Reagan used his electoral mandate to push an enormous tax cut through Congress. Individual taxpayers had their taxes cut by 25 percent over three years and, in addition, received new tax breaks, including "all-savers certificates" that allowed them to receive interest on certain accounts tax free. New tax provisions, especially one allowing corporations to deduct very rapidly investments on equipment, dramatically lowered corporate income taxes. The tax cut was "historically in a category by itself," as John Witte put it.[13] It was also the high-water mark of "supply side economics," which argued that huge tax cuts would produce new revenues, because corporations and individuals would have more money to spend. That promise was not met. Federal deficits grew to record peacetime levels, and new plans for reforming the tax code began to emerge.

The next year, Sen. Bill Bradley (D-N.J.) and Rep. Richard Gephardt (D-Mo.) proposed a different kind of tax revolution. Their plan had a top individual rate of 28 percent (compared with the existing top rate of 50 percent) and a flat corporate rate of 30 percent (compared with the existing 46 percent rate). More important, the plan demonstrated that a tax system that lowered tax rates and eliminated many deductions could broaden the tax base—that is, make it fairer—and still bring in as much revenue.

Apart from these technical considerations, the Bradley-Gephardt bill had two important political effects. First, it had a strong populist appeal, an appeal to those who believed that taxpayers who could afford expensive tax advice and who could take advantage of special shelters could avoid paying their fair share of taxes. For a president like Reagan who had long preached the virtues of lower tax rates and simpler tax forms, the proposal was especially attractive. Second, Republicans feared that the Democrats, under Bradley's leadership, might monopolize the issue, build enduring political ties with voters, and undermine Republicans' hopes of maintaining control of the Senate and winning back the House of Representatives.

It was no surprise, then, that in his 1984 State of the Union address Reagan directed the Treasury Department to study ways of making the tax system more fair. A few months later the president's hand was strengthened when Walter Mondale, instead of embracing the Bradley-Gephardt tax reform plan, decided to attack the federal deficit by proposing a tax increase. Reagan campaigned on tax reform, not tax increases, and whipped Mondale in the election.

After the election the Treasury Department announced surprisingly sweeping tax reform proposals. The Treasury plan suggested reducing the fourteen existing individual income tax brackets to three, with the top rate at 35 percent instead of 50 percent. While individuals would lose many of their deductions, they would receive a $120 billion tax cut. Corporate taxes would be raised to pay for the cut, principally by eliminating many of the deductions and credits that corporate taxpayers had been using to reduce their burden. So revolutionary were the Treasury proposals, in fact, that many political observers dismissed the plan as politically impractical. But, like the Bradley-Gephardt proposal, it was an important step in making the politically unthinkable possible. It established three precepts that were to guide subsequent debate.

Precepts of tax reform

First, tax reform was to be *revenue neutral*—that is, the tax reform plan was to take in no more and no less revenue than the existing tax system. The real purpose of this precept was to prevent tax reform from being used as a tax increase to reduce the federal deficit, which then hovered around $200 billion and threatened to remain there. Revenue neutrality thus insulated tax reform from deficit politics. It also established important ground rules for the debate: any proposal—such as lowering tax rates—that would lose revenue would have to be matched by another proposal that raised enough money to pay for it. This prevented tax reform from becoming an enormous pork barrel for distributing special benefits through the tax code. Some members of Congress argued that to tackle tax reform without reducing the deficit was unconscionable, but Reagan's supporters in Congress feared that without such a ground rule tax reform would become hopelessly bogged down in side games.

Second, tax reform aimed at real *simplification*. The tax system had become incredibly complex, creating an industry of accountants, tax advisers, and financial counselors to help people fill out their tax returns—and to help some of them avoid taxes. Simplification thus meant doing away with this complexity, and that meant eliminating many popular tax expenditures. The political consequences were obvious: everyone wanted a simpler tax system, but no one wanted to give up his or her tax breaks, the real price of a simpler system. Still, tax simplification became a rallying cry for the tax reform campaign.

Finally, tax reform was to benefit principally the *middle class*. The underlying populist motivation for tax reform was the perceived injustice of the tax system: the poor had little income on which to pay taxes, the rich had tax shelters, corporations were paying less and less tax, and the middle class was stuck with the bill. Though the definition of the middle class was imprecise, the underlying political energy behind tax reform was to give a break to middle-class taxpayers.

Reforming corporate taxes

The corporate income tax system was the logical place to get the revenue to finance lower rates for individuals. In the 1950s the average effective corporate tax rate—the percentage of corporate income actually paid in taxes—was about the same as the rate set in law—52 percent. Since the 1960s, however, a steady growth in tax expenditures cut the effective rate substantially. In 1963 corporations paid an average tax rate of

41.3 percent (compared with the top statutory rate of 52 percent), and it receded even further to 21.9 percent in 1984 (compared with the top rate of 46 percent). Corporations also contributed a diminishing share of federal revenues, down from 33.9 percent in 1950 to just 7.6 percent in 1984.[14] Like the Cheshire Cat in *Alice in Wonderland*, "Everything's gone but the grin," as House Budget Committee economist Van Ooms explained the corporate contribution.[15] Over the same period, individual income taxes increased from 34.8 to more than 46 percent of federal revenues.[16] Americans wanted to reverse the trend: a public opinion poll revealed that 54 percent of those surveyed favored a tax cut for individuals and more taxes for businesses.

The Treasury Department's proposal set the battle lines. The plan would reduce the corporate tax rate from 46 to 33 percent and take other steps to lower the cost of capital for investment. At the same time, many cherished tax expenditures were to be eliminated. Two of the targeted tax expenditures were tax breaks used by McIntyre's top ten to avoid paying taxes and even to receive tax rebates. One was the investment tax credit, which had existed in various forms intermittently since 1962, providing corporations with a 10 percent credit against their taxes for money spent on new equipment. The other break was the set of depreciation rules enacted as part of the Reagan administration's 1981 tax plan. Accounting procedures recommend that corporations "write off" (that is, depreciate) the cost of an investment over its useful life. If a new machine will last ten years, one-tenth of its cost should be deducted from profits each year. The 1981 tax plan, called the "accelerated cost recovery system" (ACRS, for short), allowed much quicker write-offs and thus provided substantial tax breaks for industries making large investments.

The issue here was much more significant than simply shifting more of the tax burden from individuals back to corporations. Debate centered on whether these tax expenditures should be used to revitalize American industries. For example, if obsolete and worn-out equipment made American industry less competitive, some argued, the tax code should encourage industry to make new investments. That, in fact, was the central purpose of the investment tax credit and ACRS. Some economists severely criticized this corporate tax strategy. It helped subsidize some corporate activities, penalized others that did not benefit from tax advantages, and raised very little revenue. "It's the worst of all worlds," Charles Hulten of Washington's Urban Institute argued. "We're running a de facto industrial policy with our tax code." [17] Many students of the tax system sought, quite simply, a "level playing field" that would prevent corporations from basing their decisions on the tax implications. Senator Bradley, for example, contended, "The best allocator of capital is the free market," not congressional committees writing the tax code.[18]

Many economists, however, argued that the tax code was a powerful weapon that should be used to direct investment, but they often disagreed sharply over the form that direct investment should take. Liberal economist Robert Reich, for example, contended that the federal government should use a Japanese-style approach to identify key industries for government support and give those industries special tax expenditures as an important part of the strategy.[19] Conservatives, including Kevin P. Phillips, argued that the government should not attempt to choose "winning industries" but should instead help all American businesses become more competitive. The global economy is a "combat zone," Phillips contended, and he called for special tax incentives as well as looser antitrust laws.[20] Although liberals and conservatives disagreed over just how focused such tax expenditures should be, many of them shared a strong belief that the tax code was a powerful vehicle for driving American industrial policy.

The General Electric Company's tax strategy richly illustrates the issues in the debate. In 1983 the company earned $2.4 billion in its domestic operations yet paid no federal income tax. In both 1981 and 1982, furthermore, the company earned $2 billion and received large refunds of taxes paid in previous years. How did GE do it? In part, the company made substantial investments in its own operations and received large tax breaks—both through the investment tax credit and ACRS—that helped eliminate its tax bill. Furthermore, GE created what the *Wall Street Journal* called the "ideal tax shelter." One of its divisions, the GE Credit Corporation, bought new equipment for other companies. GE leased the equipment to the companies and then, as purchaser, itself took the tax breaks for the investments. GE's manager of tax accounting, John McCoy, contended, "When a company responds to those incentives, I don't think they ought to be castigated. They ought to be applauded for carrying out the will of Congress." But while GE's stockholders certainly agreed, many critics wondered about a policy that encouraged GE to pursue tax shelters instead of ways of making its own operations more profitable.[21]

The tax rate on corporate income varied tremendously by industry, because some industries could better take advantage of tax expenditures than others. (See Table 4-1.) The average tax rate actually paid varied from −1.0 percent in chemicals and −0.5 in paper products to 35.6 percent in soaps and cosmetics and 34.8 in wholesaling. What accounted for the difference? Many tax breaks were more valuable to industries

Table 4-1   U.S. effective tax rates by industry, 1983

Industry	Percent
Aerospace	14.0
Beverages	18.7
Broadcasting	18.5
Chemicals	−1.0
Computers and office equipment	26.3
Construction	0.7
Electronics and appliances	7.4
Financial institutions	6.4
Food processing	25.9
Glass and concrete	17.5
Instrument companies	32.8
Insurance	9.9
Investment companies	9.3
Metal products	15.1
Motor vehicles	3.5
Paper and wood products	−0.5
Petroleum	21.3
Pharmaceuticals	27.2
Retailing	20.0
Rubber	19.6
Soaps and cosmetics	35.6
Telecommunications	4.8
Tobacco	33.8
Transportation:	
railroads	3.3
trucking	34.5
Utilities	7.1
Wholesalers	34.8

Source: U.S. Congress, Joint Committee on Taxation, *Study of 1983 Effective Tax Rates of Selected Large U.S. Corporations,* committee print, 1984, 22.

that made more long-term investments. Other peculiarities meant that those in the same line of business could pay greatly varying amounts of taxes. The trucking industry, for example, paid one of the highest average tax rates—34.5 percent—while railroads paid one of the lowest—3.3 percent.[22]

The corporate tax system had important effects on other businesses as well. The tax laws allowed businesses to deduct the cost of season tickets and luxury skyboxes—sometimes costing as much as $100,000 each—for professional sports events. One study argued that corporations accounted for 60 percent of the gate receipts at National Hockey League games, 51 percent for the National Basketball Association, and 46 percent for Major League Baseball.[23]

Tax reform thus predictably meant many different things to different industries. Firms benefiting from the existing system saw tax reform as a threat, while those paying the highest taxes saw a need to make the tax system fairer. Strongest support for tax reform, not surprisingly, came from the labor-intensive service sector and producers of consumer goods paying the highest taxes. Tax reform therefore meant making difficult trade-offs. Corporate taxes overall would have to be increased if individual taxes were to be cut. Part of the overall strategy, furthermore, was to lower the corporate tax rate. That meant tax reform would have to raise substantial revenue from corporations by eliminating many corporate deductions, both to raise money and to make the system "fairer," if, in fact, anyone could define "fairness." Every tax deduction eliminated, though, meant that someone's ox was gored. Tax reform, if it were to happen, would therefore require finding enough corporate tax revenue to balance the planned individual tax cuts. The desire for lower corporate tax rates would also have to be weighed against the general unwillingness to give up deductions.

Easing the personal tax burden

Half of the proposed $120 billion in increased corporate taxes would have to pay for taking the very poorest taxpayers off the tax rolls. The richest taxpayers, many members of Congress reasoned, had done well under the 1981 tax bill, which had reduced the top rate from 70 to 50 percent. The rest of the money, therefore, was to be focused on the middle class to help even the score and, more importantly, to help build crucial political support for tax reform. Nearly all Americans, however—92 percent by one survey—saw themselves as "middle class," with only 4 percent considering themselves "upper class."[24] With the median family income (half of the families below and half above the income level) at $26,483 in 1986, clearly the "middle income" label could not apply to everyone. There was a huge gap between taxpayers' perceptions of their situation and their true place on the income scale.

This discrepancy was a serious political obstacle for tax reform. If winning support required focusing benefits on the middle class, it obviously paid to define "middle" as broadly as possible. On the other hand, if "middle" meant nearly everyone, even $60 billion would not provide a significant tax cut for anyone. Furthermore, the strategy was to lower the tax rates but to allow fewer tax deductions. Americans in general had become very attached to their deductions, and only 35 percent of those surveyed in a public opinion poll favored limiting deductions to help pay for lower rates. Constant political debate over the deductions made Americans cynical about whether tax reform would help them personally.[25]

At the same time, most Americans supported a simpler and fairer tax system. The job of filling out the personal income tax form took 300 million hours every year, the Congressional Budget Office reported, and 40 percent of all taxpayers relied on outside professional help in completing their returns.[26] For some of the very wealthy, that help paid handsome dividends. More than 30,000 individuals making more than $250,000, and 3,000 individuals making more than $1 million, paid little or no income tax in 1983, a Treasury Department study discovered. By comparison, the average family making between $30,000 and $75,000 paid 13 percent of its income in federal income taxes.[27]

How did the rich avoid paying taxes? One quite legal strategy often used was a tax shelter in real estate, oil, or gas.[28] One taxpayer who put his money in a real estate partnership, for example, reduced his $448,000 income to a federal adjusted gross income of only $37,000 by investing $225,000 in the partnership three days before the end of the year. Thus, for a $225,000 investment for only three days, he reduced his income subject to taxes by $411,000 and his taxes to a maximum of only a few thousand dollars.

Many taxpayers, in fact, invested in shelters such as these using borrowed money. A taxpayer could take out a loan to invest in cattle, office buildings, motion pictures, oil, or gas, and then use the tax breaks from depreciation, interest expenses, and the investment tax credit to offset income from the shelter and from other sources. When the tax breaks, such as depreciation, run out, the investor can sell out and begin all over again.

Consider this strategy under pre-1987 rules. If I put up $200,000 in cash and borrow another $800,000 to invest $1 million in a partnership buying new equipment (with, for instance, a five-year life), I could deduct from my income $400,000 in depreciation in the first year. I could also deduct interest expenses for the loan (which would amount to $80,000 in the first year if I borrowed the money at 8 percent). Thus, my $200,000 investment would produce a $480,000 deduction the first year. If I sold my interest—perhaps when I could get higher deductions by investing in some other partnership—I might be able to pay the much lower capital gains tax rate on any profits. Even if the investment lost money, I might well be able to deduct the losses. Either way, I have gotten a substantial tax break on borrowed money without having taken any role in managing the investment.[29]

Tax breaks that were obviously available only to the well-to-do added to the general worries that the tax system did not treat different classes of taxpayers equally. Official tax rates rose from 11 percent for taxpayers at the bottom of the income scale to 50 percent for those at the top. The tax expenditures, however, reduced the effective income tax rate for the wealthiest taxpayers by half, to 26 percent, largely because of deductions and special treatment for capital gains and tax shelters.[30] Furthermore, taxpayers making the same amount of money often paid very different amounts of taxes, depending on the tax expenditures they could take advantage of and on their own skill in using the tax code. In Table 4-2 are listed the largest tax breaks for individuals estimated for 1986, before the passage of the reformed tax system.

Congress took aim either to reduce or eliminate three popular middle-class deductions: the special deduction for a second wage earner in a family, deductions for state and local sales taxes, and the deduction for contributions to Individual Retirement Accounts (IRAs). The proposal to end the exclusion from income for IRA contributions was an especially painful one for many middle-class taxpayers. In 1981 Congress for the first time had extended the individual retirement savings plan to all taxpayers to increase the incentives to save, both to help finance economic growth and to increase individuals' savings for retirement. A wage earner could deposit up to $2,000 per year into an

Table 4-2   Largest tax expenditures for individuals, fiscal year 1986

Tax expenditure	Revenue loss in billions
Exclusion of employer contribution to pension plan	$53.4
Preferential rate on capital gains	27.2
Home mortgage interest deduction	26.9
Exclusion of employer contribution to medical insurance	23.5
State and local tax deduction (except property tax on homes)	23.2
Deduction for interest on consumer credit	17.6
Exclusion of Individual Retirement Account contribution	14.4
Exclusion of social security benefits for retired workers	13.5
Charitable contributions deduction	11.7
Deduction for home property tax	10.1

Source: U.S. Office of Management and Budget, *Budget of the United States Government, Fiscal Year 1987, Special Analyses* (Washington, D.C.: U.S. Government Printing Office, 1986), G-42–G-46.

IRA and deduct the deposit from his or her income. The deposit and the interest it earned would not be taxable until retirement, when the tax rate would be lower. For an individual in the top 50 percent tax bracket, a $2,000 deposit really cost only $1,000, since the tax deduction produced a tax savings of $1,000. Even for a true middle-class taxpayer with a taxable income of $25,000 (in the 22 percent tax bracket), the tax savings for a $2,000 contribution was $440, which was in reality the federal government's contribution to the IRA. In the first four years of the new IRAs, 1981 to 1985, 30 million people started accounts and deposited more than $250 billion.[31]

The proposal to end or reduce IRA deductions enraged many middle- and upper-class taxpayers, who feared Congress was out to destroy the one tax break that helped them match the tax shelters of the very rich. A receptionist for Continental Telephone Company in Dallas left at her desk a petition in favor of keeping the IRA. When she returned from some errands, she discovered that the petition had attracted 160 signatures, from 80 percent of the company's employees. "This is not some campaign generated by the big banks," Al Friedricks, the company's lobbyist explained. "You want to talk about grass roots? This is it. The feeling around here, to be honest, is that the middle class is going to pay for this tax bill no matter what the politicians say, and the IRA is something that helps people in the middle." [32]

Congress, in fact, was not proposing to take the IRA away. Anyone without a company retirement plan could continue to take the IRA deduction, as could any taxpayer making less than $40,000. A partial deduction would be allowed for taxpayers making between $40,000 and $50,000, and the deduction would disappear only for taxpayers without a company retirement plan who made more than $50,000. The lower tax rates Congress planned would reduce the value of the deduction in any event, and *any* taxpayer could continue to invest in an IRA and defer taxes on the interest until retirement. It was the tax deferral on interest that was the IRA's main benefit. Furthermore, supporters of the congressional plan pointed out, upper-income taxpayers most took advantage of the IRA anyway, so ending the deduction was not going to hurt the middle class. Still, according to Friedricks of Continental Telephone, "Most people don't know much about tax reform. It's too complicated. But when it comes to IRAs, they felt like the federal legislators were reneging on a commitment to them." [33]

Thus, defining just who the middle-class taxpayers were, how much of a tax cut they ought to receive, and what tax breaks they ought to enjoy was the center of the complicated argument over revising the individual income tax. The broader the definition of middle class, the more tax breaks had to be eliminated to pay for a tax cut. Furthermore, the lower the tax rates, the more tax expenditures had to be eliminated to compensate. Fundamentally, tax reform meant deciding what broader social purposes the tax code ought to serve: redistributing income from the rich to the poor, encouraging individuals to save for their retirement, increasing incentives for families to buy homes—and on and on.

The final struggle

While the tax reform debate had a populist veneer, it was entangled in difficult partisan questions. Republicans worried that the Bradley-Gephardt proposal threatened to seize the populist issue and thus the political advantage. The Democrats feared that if Reagan were successful in pushing through his plan, his personal popularity would be further enhanced and their own position weakened. As Richard Darman, then deputy treasury secretary and a key member of the Republicans' tax reform brain trust, explained, "If they [the Democrats] didn't do something on this issue, it threatened realignment. They feared that Ronald Reagan, Jack Kemp [R-N.Y.] and the emerging populist wing of the Republican party could take away a good part" of the Democrats' traditional constituency.[34]

Both parties thus had a strong incentive to act, if for no other reason than to prevent the other side from claiming sole credit. At the same time, interest groups flooded the halls of the Capitol pressing to keep or improve every tax break imaginable. The political situation was volatile, with strong general support for the idea of tax reform but substantial opposition to many of its details. To help keep the package together, Darman worked with Republicans on Capitol Hill to frame ground rules: tax reform should remain revenue neutral and the proposals should be bundled into one package to force one up-or-down vote and prevent the plan from being picked apart.

Having announced tax reform as his major domestic priority for the second term, Reagan was not about to back off, despite his difficulty in getting Americans excited about it. He formed an unusual partnership with Rep. Dan Rostenkowski (D-Ill.), chairman of the House Ways and Means Committee. Rostenkowski did not want to abandon the issue to the Republicans, and he saw a great opportunity to build on the president's popularity to revise the tax code. The unexpected link between a conservative Republican president and a liberal Democrat from a blue-collar district was the key to steering tax reform through the House.

Within his committee, Rostenkowski's strategy sought to build a coalition of Democrats who could support a tax reform plan much like the president's. In practice, coalition-building meant keeping some of the deductions the president proposed to eliminate. With special tax breaks growing, former deputy treasury secretary Charles McLure, who helped draft the president's plan, said, "It seems to me things have substantially unraveled." No matter what shape the House plan took, he concluded, "It has become clear that whatever happens is not going to look much like tax reform." [35] Reagan did not like the package either, but on the recommendation of his advisers he finally decided to fight it no further. Any flaws, they reasoned, could be corrected in the Republican-controlled Senate. In December 1985 the House passed Rostenkowski's bill.

Packwood's proposal

In the Senate, the job fell to Sen. Robert Packwood (R-Ore.), chairman of the Finance Committee. Packwood began with Reagan's top rate of 35 percent for individuals and proposed eliminating many of the worst tax abuses, especially tax shelters. Packwood wanted to remove many of the poor from the tax rolls and to protect a favorite middle-class break, the deduction for state and local taxes. He proposed eliminating the deduction only for the wealthy. Like Rostenkowski, Packwood also traded tax expenditures, such as tax breaks for oil and gas, coal, iron ore, timber, and military contractors, for the support of different committee members.

"Every step we've taken in this process has moved further and further away from reform," one tax expert said.[36] Tax "simplification" was quickly receding with each trade. In the Senate bill, for example, the $2,000 personal exemption allowed for each dependent was to be adjusted according to the tax bracket, which would have produced a far more complex tax form than the existing one. The Finance Committee also debated limits on consumer interest deductions (for instance, for car loans) that would vary by income. Another tax accountant concluded, "This is clearly more complicated than the current system." [37]

To make matters worse, the movement for tax reform was beginning to disintegrate under the pressure of special interests. Tax reform advocates feared that by exchanging deductions for votes they were undoing the goal of reform, but they also recognized that without the deals there could be no reform at all. To stop the plan from completely unraveling, Packwood boldly switched strategies by proposing a truly radical plan based on a huge cut in income tax rates. The top rate would be cut from 50 to 25 percent compared to the top rate of 35 percent in the president's plan. So large was the rate cut that the value of any deductions would be greatly reduced as well. (If, for example, a taxpayer at the existing top rate of 50 percent took a $100 deduction, his or her taxes would be reduced by $50. If the top rate were reduced to 25 percent, the same deduction would reduce taxes by only $25, so the deduction would be far less valuable.) At the same time, everyone would benefit from the lower rates. Packwood's proposal was to slow the stampede for deductions by making them less valuable and to increase the breadth of political support by lowering everyone's rates.

The radical plan worked like shock therapy. It disrupted the deductions-for-votes trading that had dominated debate in the Senate. It called the bluff of many members of Congress who had said they favored "true tax reform," and it captured the imagination of many opinion makers who had been following the tax reform debate closely. While Packwood decided to replace a few deductions to gain needed votes on the committee, which meant that the top rate nudged up from 25 to 27 percent, he steered the bill largely unchanged through the Finance Committee. The bill curtailed most tax shelters, limited the deduction for IRAs, and upset many members of the Senate. But the Senate, faced with the revenue-neutral rule and the unwillingness of majority Republicans to derail the president's top-priority domestic program, finally passed the bill 97-3 in June 1986.

The speed with which Packwood's gambit led tax reform through the Senate—and eliminated many existing tax deductions—surprised many interest groups. Wayne Thevornot, who represented big real estate developers and syndicaters of tax shelters, conceded that "terror and disbelief is the reaction" to the tax bill's plan to end real estate tax shelters. "At least our people have nice, big buildings of their own to jump from," he said. Robert Bannister, chief lobbyist for the National Association of Homebuilders, said that the plan meant a "meltdown for housing." [38]

Bargaining in the conference committee

The final battle lines were drawn in a large twenty-two-member House and Senate conference committee assembled to reconcile the two different versions of tax reform. The House bill had a top rate for individuals of 38 percent and an increase of $142 billion in corporate taxes. The Senate bill, on the other hand, had a 27 percent top rate for individuals and an increase in corporate taxes of only $120 billion. The

Senate version treated corporations more generously, with lower rates and more deductions than the House bill. Packwood and Rostenkowski squared off, each determined not to give in to the other.

During the first weeks of August, they proved unable to reconcile their differences, and the talks broke down. Rostenkowski and his colleagues from the House were resolved to increase business taxes substantially, but many Senate conferees were committed to saving tax breaks valued by companies in their states. Senators Lloyd Bentsen (D-Texas) and Russell B. Long (D-La.), for example, wanted to save tax breaks for oil. Sen. John Danforth (R-Mo.) wanted to save special tax treatment for defense contractors in his state. As sharp as the partisan differences were, the industry-by-industry struggle over keeping tax breaks posed the bigger danger to passage of the bill. Packwood and Rostenkowski began meeting separately, but no one was really sure that, even if they could reach a compromise, their colleagues would go along. Finally, in mid-August, the tired conferees hammered out a bill on which they could agree.

The conference committee's bill leaned toward the lower rates and fewer deductions for individuals of the Senate bill and the fewer corporate loopholes of the House bill. Instead of fourteen rates for individuals ranging from 11 to 50 percent, the bill had but two rates of 15 and 28 percent. One million poor taxpayers were removed completely from the tax rolls, and $120 billion in taxes was shifted from individuals to corporations. Furthermore, the bill substantially reduced loopholes. Individuals lost the tax shelters that the wealthy had used to reduce or eliminate their tax bills. Corporations lost the rapid deductions of the ACRS and the investment tax credit.

President Reagan thus won his tax reform legislation. After announcing his plan, the president had remained outside the debate and had thereby avoided staking his personal prestige on any part of the compromise. His most important contribution, in fact, was making tax reform an issue that no one could evade and reiterating his basic position—lower tax rates and fewer deductions. He made tax reform a "dead-cat" issue.[39] No one wanted the carcass of a tax reform bill lying on his or her doorstep. Each time the plan threatened to break down, the dead-cat syndrome renewed the desire to negotiate.

Middle-class politics

The focus on the middle class kept the tax reform plan intact. After allocating enough money to remove many of the poor from the tax rolls, the bill designated about $60 billion over five years to reduce the taxes of individuals making between $20,000 and $40,000, Congress's some-what arbitrary definition of "middle class." Treasury Secretary James A. Baker III, in fact, poked fun at middle-class politics in a rap called "The Tax Reform Shuffle," a take-off of a performance by the Chicago Bears before the 1986 Super Bowl. In part, Baker's song went, "The conference met, and everybody asked/'Who can give the most to the middle class?' " [40]

Ironically, the $60 billion made little real difference in the pay-checks of most taxpayers; in the first full year of tax reform, 1988, taxes were reduced only $2.50 to $8.00 per week, on the average.[41] And 49 per-cent of those surveyed in a public opinion poll believed that the tax reform plan was unfair to the middle class, while only 45 percent believed it was fair.[42] The tax debate had been so drawn out and complicated—and citizens' cynicism was so deep—that many taxpayers did not recognize that they were likely to be better off, if only slightly. Forty-five percent of American taxpayers believed that they were likely to pay more taxes, and in April 1987 46 percent thought Congress was likely to increase the taxes they paid.[43]

The original goal of simplification disappeared with the deals struck to win the legislation's passage. Many taxpayers' calculations became more rather than less complicated because of the bill's many changes and its intricate phase-in procedure. The first experience most taxpayers had with the new law, in fact, proved a public relations disaster. The Internal Revenue Service with great fanfare released a new W-4 form designed to help taxpayers calculate how much tax should be withheld from their paychecks. For the first time in decades, every taxpayer had to fill out a new form. The form was more complicated principally because the IRS was using this opportunity to make withholding more exact, to avoid large refunds or large tax bills at the end of the year, but many citizens and politicians saw it as a symbol of betrayal. Members of Congress blasted the form in hearings, and taxpayers complained that they could not figure it out without an accountant. The uproar led IRS to release a new, simpler, and less precise W-4 form, but in the meantime public opinion against the tax "simplification" of 1986 had been poisoned.

Tax expenditures versus direct expenditures _____

When Bradley and Gephardt first suggested the idea of reducing tax expenditures in exchange for lower tax rates, few political observers believed it could—or would—come to pass any time soon. The story of the tax reform act of 1986 is one of the richest political tales of recent American history. Under the surface, though, is a deeper and much more complex message: while the 1986 tax act substantially reduced tax expenditures, it most certainly did not eliminate them as an engine of social and economic policy. In fact, as special interests and members of Congress struggled over which tax expenditures would remain, the social, economic, and political importance of tax expenditures was confirmed.

There were losers in the tax reform battle, especially individuals and corporations who had taken advantage of tax shelters to avoid— quite legally—their fair share of taxes. Industries such as real estate, steel, and banking saw themselves as big losers. Yet there were also winners. Some industries—including oil, electronics, publishing, and retailing—either kept their threatened tax breaks or improved their position because of the lower tax rates. Middle-class taxpayers, especially homeowners, also benefited. The 1986 tax bill did not end tax expenditures; rather, it redistributed the costs and benefits contained in the tax code.

The revised tax code thus continued to play an important role in guiding social policy. It discouraged both investment in IRAs and charitable giving (by reducing the value of the deduction). It also discouraged investment in real estate—investment that was fueled not by demand for new office buildings but rather by taxpayers seeking to shelter their income. It favored light industry (such as electronics) more than heavy industry (such as automobile manufacturing), because the act repealed the investment tax credit, which was used more by heavy industry.

Perhaps the most certain measure of the tax law's impact, especially in motivating taxpayers' behavior, was the explosion of year-end 1986 "beat the tax law" advertising. Television commercials urged consumers to buy new cars before the end of the year, the last year to deduct the sales tax. Charities sent mass mailings urging taxpayers to make big contributions before 1987, when the value of their deduction would be lower. In Washington, D.C., huge amounts of used clothing and even used cars (100 in one day) were donated to Goodwill Industries in the last days of 1986. Real estate lawyers were swamped by people trying to close on real estate deals by year-end, while the tax incentives for interest costs had more value than they would after 1986. Pressed by an enormous workload, a New York lawyer "snapped and totally lost it" at one closing, another lawyer present said. The witness said that the lawyer screamed obscenities, then picked up pencils and started throwing them like darts at the seller. "Thank God we hadn't ordered any pizza," the witness said. "It would have been all over the walls." And, of course, tax counselors were busier than they had been in years.[44]

Social policy making through the tax code will continue as long as there are deductions, exclusions, and credits allowed against taxes. That, in turn, is likely to continue as long as there are taxes, and there are likely to be taxes as long as there are people and governments. Furthermore, and this is a less obvious point, what can be done by a spending program can also be accomplished, often with different effects, through the tax code. As two leading students of tax expenditures, Stanley S. Surrey and Paul R. McDaniel, have written, "Any financial aid or incentive program may be written either as a tax expenditure or as a direct program."[45]

The tax code has several advantages over direct spending as an instrument of policy.[46] In a capitalist economy, creating incentives for people to act in a desired way is often more efficient than issuing orders or paying them directly. Tax expenditures usually require a smaller government bureaucracy for administration than direct spending programs. For example, the tax code has been a more powerful engine for encouraging home ownership, because of the tax deductions for home mortgage interest and property taxes, than direct grants for purchasing homes would have been.

Yet the tax code has important disadvantages. A tax expenditure is available to anyone meeting its qualifications. This means that the government cannot very precisely determine who benefits. The government has even less control over the size of the subsidy, because the total of tax expenditures used is determined by how many individuals and corporations claim which provisions on their tax returns. Unlike direct spending programs, most of which require regular appropriations, tax expenditures do not need to be reviewed once they are established. Thus, the tax expenditure strategy offers less substantive and less budgetary control. This provides a powerful motivation to make policy through the tax code when the federal deficit mounts. While increases in direct spending programs show up immediately in deficit increases, the impact of new or larger tax expenditures is less visible and direct. Tax expenditures thus are blunt policy instruments. The government has less control over the size of subsidies or who benefits from them than with direct spending programs.

Tax expenditures, furthermore, distort market choices. That, of course, is their very purpose: to encourage individuals and corporations to do things they might not otherwise be inclined to do. Still, they risk creating unintended consequences, distorting the decisions of taxpayers in ways that are neither economically efficient nor socially desirable. Do we want taxpayers to make decisions based on the tax implications of their investment or on what return the market will pay? Do we want to encourage families to own their own homes, even if that means that their housing expenses are treated differently than those of renters and even if it means that they buy larger houses than they might otherwise buy, thus steering money away from other expenditures? These questions are not easy to answer, but they are important questions to ask as we evaluate the effects of tax expenditures.

Finally, the real costs and effects of tax expenditures depend on accurate estimates of how taxpayers will use the tax code's incentives, but predicting those behaviors can be very difficult. We do not really know how much tax expenditures cost the U.S. Treasury because we do not know how taxpayers would behave in the absence of the incentives. Furthermore, analysts trying to build a "revenue-neutral" tax bill faced enormous problems because they could only guess what the effects of different provisions will be. Only after all provisions of the 1986 tax bill are in effect—after a five-year phase-in period ending in 1991—will useful estimates be possible. Compared with many direct spending programs, however, tax expenditures tend to benefit the relatively well-to-do. One needs income to claim deductions, and the more income the more deductions are worth. At the same time, the broad middle-class constituency behind the most popular expenditures has made them a fact of American political life.

At the same time, of course, direct spending programs have their own problems: maintaining government control, funding payroll costs for government employees to administer the programs, and political battling over the distribution of money. Neither direct nor indirect programs are free of problems. Rather, each has its own advantages, each its own costs. The advantages and costs revolve around these key issues: who administers the program, how Congress oversees its results, how many resources are used, and how much control—programmatic and budgetary—policy makers can exercise.[47]

Some people look on tax expenditures as "loopholes," some as natural rights, but few see them as important instruments of government policy. Still, most people think that tax expenditures ought to be used to encourage desired behavior. A 1983 survey of 600 high-level corporate executives revealed that 60 percent favored offering tax incentives to help industries become more competitive.[48] In a survey of individual taxpayers, 45 percent favored using the tax code to further social and economic goals.[49] However, rarely do policy makers weigh direct spending and tax expenditures as alternatives; rarely do they try to determine who should benefit, which will work better, which will produce fewer unintended consequences, and which will produce more public good at the least cost.[50]

The ultimate issue of the tax expenditure is recognizing it as a central policy strategy and understanding that hard choices have to be made in deciding whether to pursue tax expenditures rather than directly administered policy or one of the other government-by-proxy alternatives. The choice involves weighing complicated and often conflicting issues, directing taxpayers' behavior to desired ends, making the best use of public resources, ensuring that the public's ends are in fact served, minimizing government intrusion while maximizing individual flexibility, and maintaining confidence in government and its tax system. Quite simply, the most important means of improving the tax expenditure system is to recognize that it is in fact a policy strategy and that it deserves equal analysis and oversight—of both its intended and unintended consequences.

Notes

1. *Weekly Compilation of Presidential Documents,* May 28, 1985, 703-704, 707.
2. *National Journal,* May 3, 1986, 1059-1061.
3. Citizens for Tax Justice, "130 Reasons Why We Need Tax Reform" (Washington, D.C., July 1986), 3.
4. *Washington Post,* October 23, 1986, A1.
5. John F. Witte, *The Politics and Development of the Federal Income Tax* (Madison: University of Wisconsin Press, 1985), 75-79. See also Joseph A. Pechman, *Federal Tax Policy,* 4th ed. (Washington, D.C.: Brookings, 1983).
6. U.S. Congress, Joint Committee on Taxation, *Estimates of Federal Tax Expenditures for Fiscal Years 1984-1989,* joint committee print, 1984, 22.
7. Joel Slemrod and Nikki Sorum, "The Compliance Cost of the U.S. Individual Income Tax System," *National Tax Journal* 37 (December 1984): 461.
8. Pechman, *Federal Tax Policy,* 75, 144.
9. *National Journal,* February 2, 1985, 288.
10. *Washington Post,* March 6, 1985, A21.
11. Witte, *The Politics and Development of the Federal Income Tax,* 197.
12. Ibid., 205.
13. Ibid., 235.
14. U.S. Congressional Budget Office, *Revising the Corporate Income Tax* (Washington, D.C.: U.S. Government Printing Office, 1985), 28-29, 35-36.
15. *Wall Street Journal,* November 20, 1984, 1.
16. U.S. Congressional Budget Office, *Revising the Individual Income Tax* (Washington, D.C.: U.S. Government Printing Office, 1983), 9.
17. *Wall Street Journal,* November 20, 1984, 1.
18. *Wall Street Journal,* April 3, 1985, 1.
19. Robert B. Reich, *The Next American Frontier* (New York: Penguin Books, 1983), 241.

20. Kevin P. Phillips, *Staying on Top* (New York: Random House, 1984), 92-95.
21. *Wall Street Journal*, November 20, 1984, 1.
22. U.S. Congress, Joint Committee on Taxation, *Study of 1983 Effective Tax Rates of Selected Large U.S. Corporations*, committee print, 1984, 20-21.
23. *Wall Street Journal*, July 17, 1985, 31.
24. *Washington Post*, August 24, 1986, A4.
25. *Wall Street Journal*, June 6, 1986, 27.
26. Congressional Budget Office, *Revising the Individual Income Tax*, 2.
27. *Wall Street Journal*, August 2, 1985, 34.
28. Pechman, *Federal Tax Policy*, 124-125.
29. Derived from ibid.
30. Ibid., 75.
31. *Washington Post*, June 2, 1986, A4.
32. Ibid.
33. Ibid.
34. *New York Times*, October 26, 1986, Sec. 3, 6.
35. *Wall Street Journal*, November 6, 1985, 64.
36. *Wall Street Journal*, April 7, 1986, 54.
37. *Washington Post*, April 18, 1986, A9.
38. *Wall Street Journal*, May 8, 1986, 27.
39. *Washington Post*, June 29, 1986, A12.
40. *Washington Post*, September 17, 1986, A23.
41. *Washington Post*, August 18, 1986, A1.
42. *National Journal*, October 18, 1986, 2528.
43. *National Journal*, January 10, 1987, 96; *Washington Post*, April 15, 1987, D3.
44. *Washington Post*, December 31, 1986, A8; *Wall Street Journal*, December 31, 1986, 17.
45. Stanley S. Surrey and Paul R. McDaniel, *Tax Expenditures* (Cambridge: Harvard University Press, 1985), 99.
46. See ibid., 102-108.
47. Ibid., 117.
48. *Business Week*, April 18, 1983, 18.
49. *Wall Street Journal*, August 18, 1986, 1. Of those surveyed, 41 percent were opposed.
50. Compare Surrey and McDaniel, *Tax Expenditures*, 261.

Loans: college for everyone?

5

Secretary of Education William J. Bennett ignited a furor soon after President Ronald Reagan appointed him in 1985 when he said that many American students were being "ripped off" by colleges. "Most colleges," he argued, "promise to make you better culturally and morally, but it is not evident that they do."

At his first press conference, he announced his support for the president's proposed large cuts in federal aid to college students. Too much federal money, he suggested, was going to middle-class students attending expensive private colleges. Instead, the federal government ought to be concentrating its money on poor students who otherwise could not afford to attend. "It is not self-evident that the government has the responsibility to permit everyone to go to whatever college they want," he argued. Families might have to "tighten the belt even more," but Bennett told the reporters that he doubted that would hurt much. "It may require from some students divestiture of certain sorts: stereo divestiture, automobile divestiture, three-weeks-at-the-beach divestiture." [1]

Many students and college administrators were deeply offended. Sen. Paul Simon (D-Ill.) said that proposing students could give up three weeks at the beach to finance their education was "trivializing a very important national issue." The president of the United States Student Association, Gregory T. Moore, argued that the Reagan administration's proposals "would spell disaster for millions of students who would be forced to end their college careers." John Brademas, president of New

York University, where tuition far exceeded the administration's proposed $4,000 cap on federal aid to any individual, contended that the cuts "threaten an entire generation of scholars." [2]

Bennett vigorously defended himself. "Straight talk is what's called for. I think the stakes in education are important enough that we can't afford to be just beating around the bush," he said. "Access to higher education in the United States is one of the wonders of the world, but we cannot guarantee, and never should promise to guarantee, that whatever the cost of the college you choose, the federal government will foot the bill," Bennett concluded.[3]

The growing federal deficit was the immediate cause of Bennett's assault, but a deeper motivation was his—and the administration's—firm belief that the federal government's aid to education had grown far too large. The programs challenged by the secretary had supported a generation of college students. Middle-class and poor students, as well as colleges, had come to rely heavily on the programs. At the center of the debate were two federal loan programs—Guaranteed Student Loans (GSLs) and National Direct Student Loans (NDSLs)—that totaled $10 billion in 1986. Supporters of the loan programs argued that they cost the federal government relatively little money, considering the great number of students the programs helped. Bennett and his allies countered that the programs were troubled by ballooning costs, with the volume of GSLs alone growing more than sixfold and NDSLs nearly doubling from 1976 to 1986. The increase in defaulting on student loans raised the government's costs even more. The debate was thus about more than fiscal responsibility. The fundamental question was what the federal government's role in higher education should be and how it should use its borrowing resources to fulfill that role.

The nation's largest bank

Both student loan programs are part of an enormously complex system of federal credit. The federal government, in fact, is the nation's largest financier. Its portfolio of direct loans—loans made directly to borrowers—was $252 billion, 26 percent larger than the loan assets of the two largest U.S. commercial banks *combined*.[4] These direct loans, in turn, are only part of a federal credit system amounting to more than *$1 trillion*. (See Table 5-1.)

Federal loan programs come in three varieties. First are *direct loans* made to individuals, businesses, state and local governments, and

Table 5-1 Federal loans outstanding, 1986

	Amount in billions
Direct loans	$251.6
Guaranteed loans	449.8
Government-sponsored enterprises	453.3
Total	$1,154.7

Source: U.S. Office of Management and Budget, *Budget of the United States Government, Fiscal Year 1988, Special Analyses* (Washington, D.C.: U.S. Government Printing Office, 1987).

foreign governments. These loans help finance everything from the Commodity Credit Corporation, which provides price support loans for agricultural crops (more than $16 billion loaned in 1986), to low-rent public housing ($1.5 billion loaned in 1986). The Export-Import Bank made nearly $1 billion in loans the same year to help finance foreign trade.

Guaranteed loans are a second type. Private lenders make these loans, but the federal government guarantees their repayment. If the lender defaults on a guaranteed loan, the federal government pays the lender the lost principal and interest. In addition to the rapidly growing GSL program, guaranteed loans include other programs, such as home mortgage loans administered by the Federal Housing Administration. The FHA's loan program expanded by 175 percent from 1984 to 1985, to $47.4 billion in loans guaranteed, as lower interest rates encouraged housing construction and flooded the housing market with millions of homebuyers.

Finally, federal loan programs are administered by *government-sponsored enterprises*, quasi-public/quasi-private financial institutions. Each was created by the federal government but later became privately owned: the Federal Home Loan Banks; the Federal Home Loan Mortgage Corporation (popularly known as Freddie Mac); the Federal National Mortgage Association (also known as Fannie Mae); Student Loan Marketing Association (known as Sallie Mae); and the Farm Credit System. These government-sponsored enterprises aim to make more credit available for housing, education, and agriculture by acting as an intermediary in the lending market. They buy loans (for instance, home mortgages or student loans) from banks, package them together, and sell them to investors. This in turn frees the banks' capital to make more loans and provides the government-sponsored enterprises with more money to buy and repackage more loans. While the loans sold by these enterprises are not guaranteed by the federal government, no one believes that the federal government would allow the programs to collapse. In addition, the loans of government-sponsored enterprises enjoy special exemptions and advantages over other kinds of debt. These institutions are therefore able to borrow at rates from ½ to 3 percent less than typical corporate borrowers. These advantages have sparked rapid growth in loans—142 percent from 1980 to 1985, compared with only a 45 percent increase in corporate borrowing.

The federal government's involvement in lending programs began in 1913 with the creation of the Federal Reserve System and expanded in 1916 with the creation of Federal Land Banks. The crucial step in the expansion of federal lending, however, came in 1932, when the Reconstruction Finance Corporation was created to help make loans to businesses threatened by the Depression. The RFC established that the federal government would use its vast credit reserves to help private borrowers achieve purposes deemed to be in the public interest.[5] Over time federal lending has grown enormously, especially in guaranteed loans and in government-sponsored enterprises, and the range of "public interest" activities has likewise expanded into everything from student loans to international trade. While meaningful comparisons among the different government-by-proxy programs are difficult, since the mid-1970s loan programs have grown more rapidly than any other.

Loans as subsidies

Whatever the form or intended beneficiary, all federal credit programs have one central purpose: to allocate credit differently than the private market would. Federal loan programs are essentially *subsidy* programs, since in one way or another they seek to increase lending and lower its cost. Sometimes that subsidy comes in the form of lower rates. The federal government usually issues direct loans at much less than the market would charge, and the federal government's guarantee, in lowering the risk for lenders, usually reduces the interest rate. Federally backed loans, furthermore, often have longer repayment periods than the private sector would allow. They frequently grant borrowers deferment of interest payments and a grace period before those payments begin. In the GSL program, for example, new borrowers in 1987 committed themselves to paying 8 percent interest, substantially less than the market would have charged. Furthermore, they had a grace period ranging from six to nine months after graduation before beginning repayment, which could be spread over ten years.

The real value of this subsidy is unknown, because it is extremely difficult to estimate what the private market would have charged for the loans without the federal government's involvement. Some estimates put the subsidy for direct loans at about $10 billion and for federal loans overall at $16 billion. A careful study by Brookings Institution economists demonstrates, furthermore, that the subsidies vary greatly by program, from very little in government-sponsored enterprises to between 50 and 100 percent for student and some housing loan programs. Each of these subsidies costs money that could be used in other, competing programs, but without a systematic way of measuring these costs in the government's budgeting process, such comparison is impossible.[6] Joseph R. Wright, Jr., deputy director of the U.S. Office of Management and Budget, contends, "We make a big mistake by not having an accurate idea of the subsidy component."[7]

Controlling credit

Since 1980 Congress and the president have used a "federal credit budget" to try to manage the supply of federal credit. The intention was to budget and appropriate federal credit assistance the same way Congress appropriates regular spending programs. However, only 55 percent of the programs are actually covered by the credit budget, and the budget measures loan totals, not subsidy costs. The limits in the credit budget, therefore, have had little bite. Most ceilings are high enough to limit the growth of credit, and when popular programs reach the amount budgeted political pressures inevitably lead to higher ceilings. In 1986, for example, the Federal Housing Administration reached its lending limit. The outcry from potential homeowners was so strong that after two weeks of chaos in the housing industry Congress passed a new, higher limit and rushed a copy of the bill to President Reagan at the Tokyo economic summit for signing.

The problem of controlling credit programs is compounded by a mistaken belief that the programs cost the federal government little. The federal budget lists only net outlays: loans made minus loans repaid. This accounting grossly understates the amount of loan activity, especially for old programs collecting substantial repayments, and encourages the programs' many supporters to look at them as free.[8]

Even if the federal government did want to budget for credit, measuring the amount of credit would be hard. Suppose that the federal government wanted to aid farmers, who could get private loans at 12 percent interest. The federal government lends out a total of $1 billion at an interest rate of 8 percent. What is the program's cost? We might respond that the cost is $1 billion, the amount of the loans. We might argue that it is $1 billion less any repayments received this year. (This is the approach the federal government now uses.) We might argue that the cost is 4 percent of the unpaid balance each year, the difference between the public and private borrowing rates. Each approach can be correct, depending on the analyst's position.[9] If it is hard to measure the value of credit, it is even harder to control its growth. The lack of any consistent, effective way of measuring or controlling federal credit programs predictably has fueled their growth. When deficits grow and budget cutting becomes more urgent, furthermore, it is always tempting to replace pared spending programs with federal loan programs to do the same job. As Rep. Bill Gradison (R-Ohio) put it, federal loans are a "technique used during periods of budget stringency to do good things where the cost doesn't show up until later." [10]

The expansion of federal credit programs has very real costs. Defaults grew substantially in the mid-1980s—about 15 percent per year—and cost $6 billion in fiscal year 1985. The number of defaults varies greatly by program. Within the Farmers Home Administration, for example, 70 percent of $6.8 billion in direct loans to farmers in the mid-1980s were delinquent for three years or more. At the same time, only one-tenth of a percent of the administration's community facilities loans were in default. The federal government also faces "contingent liabilities"—potential problems that the federal government is obliged to make good—of $3 billion, including $2.3 billion in federal deposit insurance and $613 million in guaranteed loans. [11]

Federal loan programs, furthermore, have important effects on the private sector. The programs tend to shift the supply of credit toward federally subsidized programs and away from unsubsidized programs, where credit is either unavailable or available only at higher costs. The programs, in addition, tend to "crowd out" private-sector loans. Some analysts estimate that each $1 billion in guaranteed loans crowds out between $736 million and $1.3 billion in private investments. Overall, these programs tend to increase demand for credit, reallocate its use, and increase costs for borrowers not subsidized by federal programs.[12]

Federal loan programs thus have substantial effects but largely evade accountability. Said Gradison, "Skirting budget scrutiny, congressional supporters of off-budget programs can push for and expand programs without being held publicly accountable for the costs. Likewise, the president can run programs without having their costs add to the deficit. Consequently, program administrators are under little pressure to minimize costs or assess risks properly." [13] The same arguments led the Hoover Commission on the management of the federal government to contend in 1955 "that lending or guaranteeing loans is a function which the government should undertake only when private enterprise cannot or will not perform the function, and then only in furtherance of a justifiable government purpose." [14] The Reagan administration applied the commission's philosophy in reducing total federal lending and finding better ways of budgeting the loans. The twin pressures of a growing budget deficit and the administration's desire to reduce the size of government led to several proposals. In March 1987, for example, the administration asked Congress for authority to pursue two new plans. First, the administration wanted to sell direct loans to the public, so the government could accurately gauge the size of the subsidy. The loans would have to be sold at a premium to make them attractive enough to private investors, and the price difference between the loan's cost and its sales price would measure the subsidy. Second, the administration wanted to require federal agencies to buy private insurance for guaranteed loans. The cost of the insurance would help the government measure the risk and hence the subsidy value for the loans. Among the critics of the plan was House Budget Committee chairman William Gray (D-Pa.), who argued, "It's like selling your garage to pay this month's mortgage." [15]

Federal loan programs have developed in an amazing variety of public-private partnerships. As the federal government has become the nation's largest financial intermediary, its influence on the decisions of millions of individuals and corporations has grown. For few groups, however, were federal loans more crucial than for students planning how to finance their higher education.

Federal student aid

Even before World War II ended, the federal government decided that it owed returning veterans a chance for a good education. In the years since, federal student aid has grown into a complicated system of loan, grant, and work study programs.

Two key questions arose within the system of federal education aid. First, who should *benefit* from federal aid? How should the aid be distributed between the poor and the middle class? There has been near-unanimity that lower income citizens should receive substantial aid, but many federal programs have become so popular with middle-class families that cutting them back has drastic political consequences. Second, who should *pay*? Is education a public good from which everyone benefits, and therefore should the federal government pay? Or is it of more specific benefit to the individual student, who should then shoulder most of the cost? Liberals have tended to argue for heavier support by the federal government, while conservatives have contended that federal aid should be limited to those who need it most and that subsidies for middle-income taxpayers should be eliminated. Growing financial pressures, both from the federal deficit and increasing federal costs for defaults, sharply focused these questions during the Reagan years.

The federal aid menu

Federal aid to college students is a complex collection of six programs, two large and four small. (See Table 5-2.)

1. *Pell grants.* Named after the senator who sponsored their creation in 1972, Sen. Claiborne Pell (D-R.I.), Pell grants provide funds to lower income students to improve basic educational opportunity. Eligibility is determined by a complicated formula counting family income, assets, and size. The formula estimates how much a family can contribute to college costs, and the grant makes up the difference.

2. *Supplemental Educational Opportunity Grants.* Administered by colleges, this program provides up to $2,000 in extra grants for students in special need.

3. *State Student Incentive Grants.* This program provides matching grants to states for their own scholarship programs.

4. *College Work Study Program.* This federal grant program provides colleges with funds to subsidize part-time jobs for college students.

5. *National Direct Student Loans.* Congress originally established the NDSL program in 1958 as National Defense Student Loans. After the Soviet Union launched the first satellite into space, Congress wanted to help more students get a higher education, especially in the sciences. Since then the program has lost its national defense focus and has expanded into direct, low-interest loans to needy students. The program is financed by the federal government and administered by colleges.

6. *Guaranteed Student Loans.* The GSL program, begun in 1965, was of special interest to President Lyndon B. Johnson. Johnson

had borrowed to attend college, and he thought that loans should be more readily available to students. The program picked up extra support from some members of Congress anxious to derail a college tuition tax credit, a tax expenditure program that had passed the Senate in the previous year. Its supporters intended GSLs to provide minimally subsidized loans for the middle class. (Lower income students would be covered by the more heavily subsidized NDSL program.) GSL's guarantees were designed to encourage the banks to lend to college students, who often had great difficulty applying for loans because they lacked credit histories.[16]

This large menu of student aid meant that many students had to combine aid from a host of sources to be able to finance college tuition. One needy student attending a private college in New York, in fact, was an "independent student" in 1983, since her mother was dead, her father was unemployed, and she was financially on her own. Her tuition, fees, and other expenses in her senior year amounted to almost $9,000, and she pulled together a complicated financial package: a $1,700 Pell grant, a $2,500 GSL, a $500 NDSL, a $1,800 Tuition Assistance Program grant from New York state, a $1,500 scholarship from her college, and $800 from summer earnings. Such a wide-ranging collection has become commonplace for many of the nation's college students.[17]

Table 5-2 Federal student aid programs

	Dollars (in millions)	*Awards (in thousands)*
Pell grants	$3,567	2,619
Supplemental grants	379	689
State incentive grants	145	264
Work study	662	753
Direct student loans	829	896
Guaranteed Student Loans	8,156	3,433
Total	$13,738	8,654
Total number of students aided:	5,132,000	

Source: U.S. Office of Management and Budget, *Budget of the United States Government, Fiscal Year 1988, Appendix* (Washington, D.C.: U.S. Government Printing Office, 1987), I-I14.

The Guaranteed Student Loan program

The GSL program has grown rapidly since 1978, when the federal government removed income limits on eligibility for the loans. In just one year, from 1978 to 1979, the number of participants increased 39 percent while the amount borrowed grew 52 percent. From fiscal 1979 to 1981, loans mushroomed from $3 billion to $7 billion.[18] In the meantime, GSLs have become the largest federal student aid program, with 3.6 million students borrowing $8.3 billion in fiscal 1986. Precise statistics on who borrows how much money, however, are very difficult to get. The program is administered by lending agencies in each state, and no data have been collected on the combined borrowing from different programs. Thus, while federally supported lending for higher education is unquestionably large—about $10 billion in 1986—firm statistics are impossible to come by.[19]

The program's growth is easily explained: it is attractive to nearly everyone. Bankers receive "special allowances" to subsidize the difference between the student's repayment rate (between 7 and 9 percent in the mid-1980s) and the market cost of money. The federal government pays all of the interest while the student is in school and guarantees repayment if the student later defaults. Furthermore, Sallie Mae—the Student Loan Marketing Association—has the special borrowing privileges that all government-sponsored enterprises enjoy. It buys loans from banks and resells them to private investors. Because these loans are nearly risk free, Sallie Mae can borrow at very favorable rates. This increases the amount of money available for lending to students and creates a very profitable business for banks.[20] As Edward A. Fox, president of Sallie Mae, put it, "Instead of the lenders making these loans out of a little pot of 'do-good money,' they are part of the banks' regular business operations."[21]

For students, GSLs are a source of cheap loans for individuals who otherwise might not be able to borrow at all. The federal government not only pays the interest while the student is enrolled but also allows a grace period after studies end before a student must begin repaying the loan. Furthermore, GSLs provide borrowers with a reasonably generous repayment schedule. In 1987 students could borrow up to $10,000 for four years of college (and up to $25,000 including graduate school) and faced repayment of between $50 and $203 per month, with repayment stretched up to ten years.

The program is scarcely free, however, either for students who must repay the loans or the federal government that must pay for the subsidies attached to the program and for the increasing number of defaults.

Costs to students

Even more dramatic than the dollar growth of GSLs has been the growth in the number of borrowers under the program. Nearly one-third of the 14 million students annually enrolled in higher education borrow from one of the federal loan programs, and somewhere between one-third and one-half of all students emerge from school with some kind of debt. The average burden of students from public colleges is $6,685—in private colleges a much higher $8,950—but these amounts vary enormously among students.[22]

The dollar volume of GSLs in 1986, in fact, was eight times larger than in 1971. However, the real growth in federal aid has come from the increase in the number of borrowers. (See Table 5-3.) In constant dollars, the average loan was 17 percent smaller in 1986 than in 1971. There were three and one-half times more participants, and nearly three times more money borrowed in 1986. Consequently, the debt burden for

Table 5-3 Volume of student loans

	1970-1971	1985-1986
Guaranteed Student Loans		
Number of loans	1,017 million	3.640 million
Dollars loaned		
current dollars	$1.015 million	$8.288 million
constant 1986 dollars	$2.872 million	$8.493 million
Average loan		
constant 1986 dollars	$2,824	$2,333
National Direct Student Loans		
Number of loans	452 million	854 million
Dollars loaned		
current dollars	$240 million	$751 million
constant 1986 dollars	$680 million	$770 million
Average loan		
constant 1986 dollars	$1,505	$902

Source: Janet S. Hansen, "Student Loans: Are They Overburdening a Generation?" Report prepared for U.S. Congress, Joint Economic Committee (Washington, D.C.: photocopied, 1986), 8.

college students has not increased dramatically, but the use of the GSL program has. As policy analyst Janet S. Hansen concluded in a report prepared for Congress's Joint Economic Committee, "Perhaps more important than total debt levels for undergraduates is the fact that borrowing is now so much more common." [23]

What is the source of this dramatic increase in borrowing? In part, Congress has cut spending for federal grant programs—especially Pell grants—and students have relied on GSLs to take up the slack. In the first years of the Reagan administration, from fiscal years 1981 to 1985, Pell grants decreased 5.7 percent (after allowing for inflation) while GSLs increased 10.8 percent.[24] In academic year 1975-1976, grants accounted for 80.3 percent of federal aid to education, while loans amounted to only 16.9 percent. Ten years later, grants and loans were nearly even, at 47.8 percent and 48.8 percent of federal aid respectively.[25] Pell grants must be appropriated by Congress, while GSLs carry an automatic entitlement for any student who qualifies. Students from families making less than $30,000 automatically qualify, and students from families with higher incomes might be entitled to GSLs if they meet the program's needs test. The volume of loans in any year thus cannot be controlled, except by changing the eligibility requirements. In addition, the GSL changes that Congress made in 1978 increased banks' willingness to lend money to students.

In the meantime, the GSL program has expanded substantially into higher education programs lasting two years or less (principally at community colleges and technical and trade schools). Furthermore, as federal grants have decreased, many more students from lower income families are relying on GSLs. In 1983 nearly 40 percent of all participants came from families earning less than $15,000 (at a time when the median family income was $24,580). Another 27.1 percent of the participants came from families earning between $15,000 and $30,000.[26] As Hansen concluded, "As GSL has evolved over 20 years, it has changed from a minimally-subsidized loan of convenience for middle-income students to a high-subsidized loan for students who can demonstrate financial need." [27]

Two long-term issues are of central concern to student borrowers: the effects of substantial borrowing on students' future creditworthiness and the effects of more borrowing for the disadvantaged.

The loan burden. Some studies of the GSL program have warned that the increase in lending would make it harder for students to borrow for other purposes in the future, for home mortgages and consumer goods, for example.[28] However, the average student loan has stayed about the same and the repayment burden thus has not increased. (See Table 5-3.) The size of students' debts does not seem to impair most borrowers.[29]

This debate on students' creditworthiness, though, hides a more basic issue. Students typically borrow to help get better jobs than they could otherwise. They cannot know, however, how much money they will make and, therefore, what their actual burden in repaying student loans will be.[30] That means the real risk in student aid is not the growing debt burden for students. It is, rather, that more and more students are assuming such a burden without knowing their future ability to repay. For a significant number of students, especially among the already disadvantaged, that gamble might not pay off.

Loans and the disadvantaged. The expansion of GSLs has come in substantial part from more borrowing by traditionally disadvantaged groups—lower income students, minorities, and women—who usually earn less than white males in equivalent jobs. They tend to borrow more than in the past yet typically have lower incomes from which to repay their obligations. Hansen argued that even adjusting for differences in education and work experience, these groups "will find loans more burdensome to repay. In this sense, loans, unlike grants, are not neutral in their effects on different groups." [31]

The shift from grants to loans thus demonstrates an important issue of government by proxy. Grants and loans can produce similar bene-fits—federal aid to students pursuing higher education. In that sense, the strategies are interchangeable. They do not, however, have similar costs. Hansen explains that "the federal strategy for fostering equality of opportunity in higher education, which initially focused on a balanced array of grants, loans, and work opportunities for the disadvantaged, has been transformed, with uncertain and largely unexamined implications for the groups who were the original focus of federal concern." [32] Grant programs lower the costs of higher education regardless of a student's ability to pay. The burden of loans, on the other hand, depends on repayment and hence on a student's income after leaving school.

As the underlying issues in the debate on reducing the federal government's costs show, that repayment burden often varies dramatically.

Costs to the federal government

Like all federally sponsored loan programs, GSLs enjoy a substantial government subsidy. As with other subsidies, the size is hard to determine, but some studies have put the value of the loan guarantee (and the lower rates it produces) at from 40 to 50 cents per dollar lent, which in 1986 meant a $4 billion to $5 billion subsidy.[33] Furthermore, Sallie Mae's special borrowing privileges produced, according to the Congressional Budget Office, another subsidy of about $40 million.[34] The subsidy is central to the GSL program: its goal is to reduce students' borrowing costs.

Especially during the early 1980s, however, abuse of the subsidy became a major source of embarrassment to program officials. Inflation had driven interest rates in the private market to record levels, and GSL rates were less than half the 18 to 20 percent that investors could earn on common investments, such as money market funds. Some families borrowed as much as possible and used the money either for investments or in place of borrowing—at much higher rates—for other purposes. GSLs "quickly became a source of money for a lot more than tuition," as Denis P. Doyle and Terry W. Hartle put it. *House and Garden* magazine, for example, recommended that parents use student loans to finance home improvement projects.[35] To make matters worse for the loan programs, stories about the use of educational loans for noneducational purposes appeared at the beginning of the Reagan budget cuts and enraged many public officials and private citizens.

The problem diminished greatly as private-sector interest rates dropped in the mid-1980s—and as the spread between these rates and the GSL rate decreased greatly. But the question remained: how much federal subsidy should be concentrated on poor families as opposed to relatively better-off middle-class families? For that matter, should federal loans, especially to middle-class families, be subsidized at all?

Defaults on student loans

Questions about the program grew even more serious as GSL defaults threatened to increase. Education Secretary Bennett estimated that the default rate would rise from 10.7 percent of borrowers in 1984 to 13.9 percent in 1990, an "alarming" increase. Defaults cost the federal government more than $1 billion in 1985, compared with $749 million in 1984. "Ultimately," Bennett argued, "the costs of a high default rate by current students must be borne by the taxpayers and by students seeking loans in the future." [36]

The default problem comes partly from the enormous increase in borrowing. Of all student loans the federal government had guaranteed up to 1984, 64 percent were made between 1981 and 1984. Furthermore, 62 percent of all federal loans ever made had reached maturity from 1982 to 1984. Defaults increased dramatically but the default rate remained about the same; the huge increase in the *number* of borrowers, not the *rate* at which they defaulted, produced the problem. Most borrowers who fall behind in their payments, moreover, eventually do repay. Thus, the program's proponents point out that the increase in federal spending for defaults is largely a product of the large growth in borrowing—and that the federal government eventually recovers a substantial part of this money.[37]

The default problem also can be attributed to *who* borrows. Many studies, in fact, suggest that a majority of defaulters come from poor families. In a Virginia survey, more than half of the defaulters had a family take-home income of less than $10,000. One defaulter with an annual income of $8,000 told the investigators, "It really makes me uneasy not being able to pay back my loan, or complete my education. It's very hard to light a candle without a match." [38] The lower a person's income, the harder it is to pay off the loans.

We often assume that students who borrow the most money are most likely to default. However, some analysts argue that increasing federal expenditures for loan defaults is a product of more borrowing by "high-risk" students, especially the poor and disadvantaged, attending "high-risk" institutions such as community colleges and trade schools. Defaults tend to be most frequent among students who stay in school only one or two years and who do not obtain a degree or certificate. Among these students, finding a job is often more difficult and the income they earn is likely to be lower than that of students who attended four years of college. "The total amount of indebtedness incurred," policy analyst Hansen points out, "appears to be much less a factor in default than does the relationship of this indebtedness to later income, the prospects for which are poorer for dropouts than for graduates and for students who attain higher levels of schooling." [39]

Thus, defaults occur most frequently among holders of small loans. The average balance upon default is $2,668, just a little more than the one-year maximum loan in 1987 of $2,500. Students with larger balances tend to be in school for more years, and thus have better chances of finding jobs paying higher salaries. The link to default seems to have less to do with the institution than with the economic status of the student. Pennsylvania GSL official Jerry S. Davis argued that "no less than one out of every three defaulting borrowers comes from an extremely limited financial circumstance." Such students are more likely to attend the kinds of institutions with the highest default rates. In California, for example, the default rate for students who attended four years of college was 8.2 percent; for two-year private colleges, 14.1 percent; for community colleges, 23.6 percent; and for vocational schools, 24.6 percent. In

111

Virginia, students with fewer than two years of higher education took out 18 percent of all loans but accounted for 51 percent of defaults. And in a national study, 38.2 percent of defaulters attended school for only one year; in Pennsylvania and Virginia the share was 50 percent and in New York, 66 percent.[40]

The default problem thus seems to be a problem of the borrower's prospects, which stem from his or her background. As federal grant programs have shrunk, more students—especially more low-income and minority students—have tended to borrow. They often attend programs lasting two years or less, sometimes drop out without finishing the program, and have a harder time finding good jobs and earning a salary high enough to repay their loans.

To be sure, there are some borrowers who try to cheat the government by refusing to repay their loans. A federal survey in 1983 identified 46,850 federal government employees who had defaulted. The government began an aggressive program of contacting these employees, arranging for repayment, and if all else failed, deducting up to 15 percent of their paychecks for repayment.[41] The typical defaulter, however, is someone who has borrowed relatively little, has had few years of higher education, comes from a lower income family, and earns relatively little money. Thus, at the core of the default problem is the stark inability to pay.

Reforms

The constant drumbeat of stories about abuses, from middle-class families borrowing to finance home improvements to thousands of students defaulting on their loans, has led to recurring attacks on the program. Critics, furthermore, have argued that the easy availability of loans tends to increase the costs of higher education. Education Secretary Bennett charged that "colleges raise costs *because they can,*" adding that "a very important factor in that ability to raise costs has been the availability of federal student aid."[42]

In fact, college tuition in the 1980s did increase faster than the cost of living. From 1980 to 1986, consumer prices increased 31 percent while tuitions rose 77 percent. However, the colleges were catching up from the inflationary 1970s, when tuition had lagged substantially behind inflation. Tuition increased 90 percent in that period while the cost of living more than doubled, rising 114 percent. Furthermore, during the 1970s federal student aid rose 313 percent while during the early 1980s it increased only 17 percent. Colleges thus tended to increase tuition more slowly while inflation was highest and federal aid increased rapidly.

When both federal student aid and inflation slowed, colleges increased tuition to make up the difference. "Given this, it requires a considerable act of faith to believe that federal aid pushes up college costs," as two education policy experts argued.[43]

There nevertheless is a pervasive sense of uneasiness about the GSL programs. The College Scholarship Service tried in December 1985 to produce recommendations for reform by calling together more than fifty loan experts: educators, bankers, state guarantee loan officers, and students. "Somewhat to the organizers' surprise, however, there was no consensus among those in attendance about what the 'problem' was, or even if there *was* a problem," wrote policy analyst Hansen.[44]

The GSL "problem" tends to revolve around questions of values. Should the federal government subsidize loans for middle-class college students, who tend to have the best prospects upon graduation? Should the federal government instead concentrate more of its resources on the poor and disadvantaged?

And these questions lead to other issues. On the one hand, defaults on loans are less likely if loans are made only to low-risk students—those who offer the most promise for high salaries on graduation. On the other hand, if the government decides to concentrate larger subsidies on the disadvantaged, it naturally risks higher rates of default, since these students can less afford to stay in school, usually attend school for fewer years, and often make less money on graduation. Such loans are riskier—and the assumption of such risks is the very purpose of the GSL program. Making loans to the least risky students thus tends to cost the government less. There is a clear trade-off between the federal interest to concentrate limited resources where they will make the most difference and the government's desire to protect itself from default.

Secretary Bennett in 1986 announced one proposal to deal with this trade-off. Ten colleges would begin a new experimental loan program, in which taxpayers would no longer subsidize the interest rate. Nine months after leaving school the borrower would begin repaying the loan at the market rate, but the monthly payment would never exceed 15 percent of the borrower's income. Bennett hoped this plan would ensure that students' resources were never unduly strained by their repayment burden. A Reagan White House spokesman argued, "Students are the principal beneficiaries of their investment in higher education. It is therefore reasonable to expect them—not taxpayers—to shoulder most of the costs of that investment." Some educators sharply disagreed. Richard F. Rosser, president of the National Association of Independent Colleges and Universities, contended, "It can only result in fewer

113

students taking out loans, fewer students going to college, or students going to the cheapest institutions." [45]

The federal government moved at the same time to tighten eligibility standards for GSLs in an effort to limit the program to the poorest and most needy students, a definite break from the program's original aims. Virginia officials estimated that the restricted standards might cut as many as 30 percent of previous loan recipients from the program. In Pennsylvania, education officials said that 20 percent of their students stood to lose federal GSLs and 30 percent more would receive smaller loans because of the cuts.

More than a dozen states, however, filled the gap by establishing their own guaranteed loan programs, aimed at students from higher income families. Although many students thus found a new source for their education loans, the new programs introduced a new twist. State governments began taking on the wealthier, and hence the least risky students, while the federal government sought to concentrate its aid on poorer students who were most likely to default. The switch illustrated the often-complex interrelationships among federal, state, and local proxy programs. The federal government risked assuming an even larger burden for the riskiest students—and further weakening federal support for the GSL program—while passing on to the states the low-risk students.

The debate is largely a philosophical one about the government's proper role in financing education. What should be subsidized? Who should benefit? What form should the subsidies take: grants, which do not discriminate in their effects according to the student's income; or loans, which offer much more subsidy for the dollar but can have very different effects depending on a student's eventual income? Furthermore, the very nature of programs like GSL means that the costs of their subsidy are often hidden and that control over the subsidy is extremely unreliable. The loan version of government by proxy, therefore, offers very perplexing philosophical and administrative problems.

The farm loan crisis _____

In even bigger trouble, both economic and political, than the GSL program was the nation's system of farm credit. In 1985 and 1986 the Farmers Home Administration (FmHA), another of the government-sponsored enterprises that packages and sells government loans, lost nearly $5 billion in defaulted loans. Of all FmHA borrowers, 36 percent were delinquent on loans, and four of five delinquent loans were overdue for more than three years. In the Farm Credit System—a federally backed system of private, cooperatively owned lenders—one-fourth of the loans were either foreclosed or listed as "high risk." [46] "Rural America is just shot," Hap Arnold, a banker and farm implement dealer in Charleston, Mississippi, noted sadly, as he struggled with rising defaults by customers.

What caused the problem? For years farmers had been counting on ever-higher land prices against which they could borrow to support and expand their farms. With the 1981 recession, however, farmers entered a dangerous cycle. The prices of many crops dropped—partly because of very good yields—so farmers could not raise enough money to repay their loans. In Minnesota, for example, farmers were paid only $2 for a bushel of corn that cost $3.40 to produce. At the same time the value of farmland plummeted, so farmers had fewer assets to sell to reduce their debt.[47] As Dorothy Lau, a Nebraska farmer, explained, "We tried to borrow ourselves out of debt. That's what happens when you don't get a price for commodities." She concluded, "Credit has replaced price as our way of doing business." The federal government supported much of that credit.[48]

For many farmers it seemed an inescapable trap. Credit is a central part of farming: farmers typically borrow money to buy the seed, fertilizers, and equipment needed to plant their crops and then use the fall proceeds from the fall harvest to repay the loans. In 1986, however, 5 percent of the nation's 2.2 million farmers could not find a lender to finance their spring planting. More than 15 percent of the farmers in Texas told state agriculture officials that they expected 1986 to be their last year in farming.[49]

The farm credit system's huge losses and the federal budget deficits prompted the Reagan administration and many members of Congress to pressure the system to get tougher with defaults and to operate more like a private lender. Yet members of Congress from farm states argued that the government was being too tough on farmers. Douglas Sims, president of the Farm Credit Banks in St. Louis, said, "We're caught between being told to run the system like a business, and that we aren't being lenient enough with farmers." A member of the House Agriculture Committee's staff, Robert Cashdollar, added, "The farmers are having hard times and the lenders are having hard times, which makes for hard politics." [50]

Under pressure to recoup delinquent loans, FmHA hired private collection agencies to contact farmers. The letters one New Jersey firm mailed read in part, "This claim has been sent to us for immediate collection. Send us full payment at once!" The letters demanded full payment in ten days. Many farmers were outraged. Some received letters in spite of having worked out repayment agreements. Some had already forfeited the collateral they had put up for the loans and were insulted that they were subjected to such pressure again. Others simply found they could not, after being delinquent for several years, scrape together the money they owed in just ten days. FmHA administrator Vance Clark acknowledged, "There is, sadly, the perception that we are moving in an unsympathetic, bureaucratic fashion against those who have suffered the most as a result of economic problems in American agriculture and who are least able to make payments." [51]

Experiment in Minnesota

Federal lending agencies faced a real dilemma: how to collect the money farmers owed without worsening the plight of the farmers. There were several approaches to dealing with the farm credit problem. One, of course, was foreclosure, in which the lender sought to take possession of the farmers' collateral—usually the farm itself. Another was bankruptcy, in which a farmer declared himself insolvent. In some hard-hit states farmers suggested a mortgage foreclosure moratorium that would deny lenders the right to court action against the borrowers. One Minnesota farmer arguing for the moratorium said it was critical to "put the squeeze on lenders." The lenders naturally found the proposal unacceptable.[52] All of the strategies were expensive and time consuming—and in the end typically left neither side satisfied. The only simple answer— raising commodity prices—was impossible.

Minnesota officials experimented with a voluntary moratorium program that had only limited success. The program was only three sentences long and, farmers argued, had many loopholes. It was voluntary—banks could choose whether or not to participate. Furthermore, it dealt only with mortgage loans backed by land. Farmers who had put up their cattle or machinery or already entered foreclosure proceedings were not covered. One attorney for a farm protest group argued, "This thing's got more holes in it than Swiss cheese." [53]

In March 1986 Minnesota moved from the moratorium to an innovative mandatory mediation system. The mediation plan follows a very simple procedure. When a creditor decides to foreclose on a farm debt of more than $5,000, the creditor must offer the farmer fourteen days to contact the local agricultural extension office and arrange for mediation. The office appoints an independent mediator—sometimes someone with experience in agricultural lending and more often a volunteer specially trained for the work—who then usually brings together all of the farmer's creditors to see if some arrangement can be made. No foreclosures can be made during mediation.

Nothing forces the different sides to reach agreement. Moreover, the deceptively simple process hides the deep disputes inherent in the farm crisis. When a banker under heavy financial pressure confronts a near-bankrupt farmer in danger of losing both land and home, emotions run high, and resolution is extremely difficult. Doug Peterson, a Minneapolis lawyer who worked nearly a day per week as a negotiator, said he had been "struck by the remarkable willingness of all concerned to cooperate with each other. They feel it's a waste of time to lay blame" for the farm credit crisis.[54]

Farmers were almost universally happy with the mandatory program. Many bankers, however, were concerned about the delays, costs, and red tape that the program added to the process of debt collection. The state's largest agricultural lender, in fact, filed suit in federal court charging that the program was unconstitutional. Nevertheless, some bankers were more happy with the results. The dean of the Agricultural Extension Service, Patrick Borich, noted that some lenders said privately that "they feel quite positive about the results. It's working better than they feared." Despite their different perspectives, the antagonism between farmers and creditors seemed remarkably low.

A negotiated solution

For Minnesota farmers, the plan worked better than any other alternative. In the program's first eleven months, the mediations produced 1,490 settlements, and another 456 cases were solved outside negotiation.[55] Most of these settlements allowed the farmers to stay in business by stretching out the repayment period. As one county agricultural agent pointed out, "When you consider that all the cases were looking at foreclosure, the program is a success." Not all of the cases reached a successful conclusion, for sometimes the lender and borrower could not find common ground. One mediator explained that the hardest part of the process was "when you realize that there's nothing that can be done, that you can't help." Still, the program proved so attractive that Iowa started a mandatory mediation program, while Wyoming, Oklahoma, Utah, South Dakota, Kansas, and Wisconsin adopted voluntary programs. In many farm states, mediation helped defuse the crisis atmosphere that had developed in farm credit.

Mediation programs are clearly not a long-term solution to the crisis. Some farmers, no matter how hard they try or how much effort negotiators apply, will never be able to repay their loans. Furthermore, the negotiating sessions are costly, especially to the lender who often has already waited several months to begin seeing the money owed and then must agree to a longer repayment period. Nevertheless, the program offers real promise. Every successful negotiation is a default and foreclosure avoided. That, in turn, saves the government money in making good on loan guarantees or writing off direct loans as losses. It ensures that lenders will eventually be able to collect their money instead of taking possession of less valuable farmland or used farm equipment. Negotiation is also many farmers' best hope of staying in business, sometimes on farms that have been in their families for generations.

Critics of the management of federal loan programs often urge that they be "run more like a business." But the very purpose of these loans is to make loans that private business would not. Borrowers under federal programs typically are higher risks, so repayment problems, even defaults, are more likely than ordinary loans in the private sector. Funding that risk is an implicit part of the loan program. Moreover, federally subsidized borrowers are borrowing for purposes that members of Congress and other public officials have deemed in the public interest, whether to get higher education or to produce crops. Federal loan programs thus are neither like private lending nor like directly administered governmental programs. Their administration requires special managerial talents, a perspective that reflects the programs' special purposes, and, often, a knack for innovative ways of resolving the inevitable disputes.

Notes

1. *New York Times,* February 12, 1985, A1, B24.
2. *New York Times,* February 19, 1985, C15; February 13, 1985, A23; February 12, 1985, B24.
3. *New York Times,* February 13, 1985, A23; February 17, 1985, Sec. 4, 20.
4. These data and the information that follows come from U.S. Office of Management and Budget, *Budget of the United States Government, Fiscal Year 1988, Special Analyses* (Washington, D.C.: U.S. Government Printing Office, 1987), F3.
5. U.S. Commission on Organization of the Executive Branch of Government (Hoover Commission), *Task Force Report on Lending Agencies* (Washington, D.C.: U.S. Government Printing Office, 1955), 1.
6. Office of Management and Budget, *Special Analyses,* F-33-34; *Washington Post,* November 20, 1986, A10; Barry P. Bosworth, Andrew S. Carron, and Elisabeth H. Rhyne, *The Economics of Federal Credit Programs* (Washington,

D.C.: Brookings, 1987), 33.

7. *National Journal,* August 9, 1986, 1946.
8. U.S. Congressional Budget Office, *New Approaches to the Budgetary Treatment of Federal Credit Assistance* (Washington, D.C.: U.S. Government Printing Office, 1984), xi; OMB, *Special Analyses,* F-6.
9. Congressional Budget Office, *New Approaches,* 1.
10. *Washington Post,* April 19, 1987, H1.
11. Office of Management and Budget, *Special Analyses,* F-39, F-45; *Washington Post,* November 20, 1986, A10.
12. James T. Bennett and Thomas J. DiLorenzo, *Underground Government* (Washington, D.C.: Cato Institute, 1983), 143-144. More generally, see Dennis S. Ippolito, *Hidden Spending* (Chapel Hill: University of North Carolina Press, 1984).
13. *Wall Street Journal,* May 15, 1984, 28.
14. Hoover Commission, *Lending Agencies,* 3.
15. *Wall Street Journal,* November 28, 1986, 1.
16. Ippolito, *Hidden Spending,* 29-33; Janet S. Hansen, "Student Loans: Are They Overburdening a Generation?" Report prepared for the U.S. Congress, Joint Economic Committee (Washington, D.C.: photocopied, 1986), 2.
17. Denis P. Doyle and Terry W. Hartle, "Student Aid Muddle," *Atlantic Monthly,* February 1986, 32.
18. *National Journal,* February 21, 1986, 312.
19. Hansen, "Student Loans," 3.
20. U.S. Congressional Budget Office, *Government-Sponsored Enterprises and Their Explicit Federal Subsidy: The Case of Sallie Mae* (Washington, D.C.: U.S. Government Printing Office, 1985), x.
21. *National Journal,* February 21, 1981, 314.
22. Hansen, "Student Loans," 9, 20.
23. Ibid., 17.
24. *Congressional Quarterly Weekly Report,* September 14, 1985, 1820.
25. Hansen, "Student Loans," 51.
26. Ibid., 20.
27. Ibid., 58.
28. See, for example, Virginia Association of Student Financial Aid Administrators, "Restoring Balance in Student Aid Programs in Virginia" (Richmond: photocopied, 1985).
29. Hansen, "Student Loans," 44.
30. Ibid., 37.
31. Ibid., 57.
32. Ibid., 58.
33. Ibid., 62; Bosworth, Carron, and Rhyne, *The Economics of Federal Credit Programs,* 149.
34. Congressional Budget Office, *Government-Sponsored Enterprises,* 33.
35. Doyle and Hartle, "Student Aid Muddle," 34.
36. *Los Angeles Times,* August 29, 1985, Part I, 2.
37. Jerry S. Davis, "Ten Facts About Defaults in the Guaranteed Student Loan Program" (Harrisburg: Pennsylvania Higher Education Assistance Agency, 1985).
38. Virginia Association, "Restoring Balance," 4.
39. Hansen, "Student Loans," 32.

Regulation: air tragedy in Newfoundland 6

Just before dawn on December 12, 1985, an Arrow Air DC-8 began its takeoff roll on an airstrip in Gander, Newfoundland. The 248 soldiers aboard were headed home to Fort Campbell, Kentucky, for the holidays with their families after a six-month tour in the Sinai desert, as part of an international peacekeeping team separating Israel and Egypt. Following the stop in Gander for refueling, the plane was on its last leg of the long trip home from the Middle East. It made it into the air but, just past the edge of the airport, the plane stalled, dipped to the right, and crashed. The just-loaded aviation fuel exploded and scattered debris from the plane over several square miles. The crash killed all 256 persons aboard—the soldiers and the plane's crew of 8—and turned a happy homecoming into a wake. "Our hearts go out to the loved ones of these brave soldiers," President Ronald Reagan said, "who have paid the fullest price in the service of their country and the cause of peace." [1]

Arrow Air was a multimillion-dollar business built on charter operations, especially to the military. It was a child of the 1978 deregulation of the nation's air service, deregulation intended to make air service cheaper and more widely available. Literally hundreds of new airline companies had sprung up since deregulation—small commuter lines ferrying passengers between small-town airports, contract carriers similar to Arrow Air, and intercontinental airlines offering unprecedented low fares.

Many aviation experts worried that the rapid growth in air service combined with the cost-cutting, no-frills policies of the new lines would

121

undermine air safety. In fact, Arrow Air's safety practices quickly became the central focus of the investigation. The plane had sat on the apron for an hour during refueling, in 25-degree temperatures with a light snow falling. The pilot decided to take off without having the plane de-iced, a costly and time-consuming process of spraying an alcohol mixture on the plane's flight surfaces. Federal regulations explicitly prohibit pilots from taking off with any snow or ice adhering to the plane (see Figure 6-1). Several other pilots took off just before the crash without having their planes de-iced, but investigators speculated that the snow and ice might have made the fatal difference for a plane heavily loaded with passengers and full tanks of fuel.

Investigators also learned, however, that Arrow Air had a long history of maintenance problems. The wife of one Army officer who had flown Arrow Air to the Sinai six months before told the *New York Times* that her husband was "extremely depressed" about having to fly the same airline home. The officer, Capt. Edward Manion, had described the aircraft as unkempt and overloaded. "It just looked sleazy," he had told his wife after arriving in the Sinai. "It lumbered and bumped and took so long to get up in the air I was surprised it got up at all." Captain Manion's premonitions were on target; he was one of the 248 soldiers killed in Gander.[2]

Federal safety regulations require airlines to maintain their planes according to minimum standards and to keep records documenting the maintenance (see Figure 6-1). By complying with these requirements, the airlines act as proxies for the government in its role as regulator.

Regulation as a policy strategy

Airline safety in the United States is the product of a complex system. The Federal Aviation Administration (FAA) prescribes minimum standards for the training of air crews, the maintenance of airplanes, and the conduct of flights. The airlines themselves are responsible for ensuring that the rules are met. They train the crews, maintain the planes, and, to demonstrate their compliance, keep formal records on each crew member and plane. FAA inspectors then check up on the work and, in particular, the records the airlines keep. The safety of the airlines thus is supported by a regulatory system, with the airlines acting as the federal government's proxies in complying with the rules.

Regulation itself is a varied phenomenon, and at the same time it is one of the most universal features of government. Regulations are the glue that holds the government together. Rules govern everything the

Figure 6-1 Federal air safety regulations

§ 125.221 Icing conditions:
Operating limitations.

(a) No pilot may take off an airplane that has—

(1) Frost, snow, or ice adhering to any propeller, windshield, or powerplant installation, or to an airspeed, altimeter, rate of climb, or flight attitude instrument system;

(2) Snow or ice adhering to the wings or stabilizing or control surfaces; or

(3) Any frost adhering to the wings, or stabilizing or control surfaces, unless that frost has been polished to make it smooth.

(b) Except for an airplane that has ice protection provisions that meet Appendix C of this part or those for transport category airplane type certification, no pilot may fly—

(1) Under IFR into known or forecast light or moderate icing conditions; or

(2) Under VFR into known light or moderate icing conditions, unless the airplane has functioning deicing or anti-icing equipment protecting each propeller, windshield, wing, stabilizing or control surface, and each airspeed, altimeter, rate of climb, or flight attitude instrument system.

(c) Except for an airplane that has ice protection provisions that meet Appendix C of this part or those for transport category airplane type certification, no pilot may fly an airplane into known or forecast severe icing conditions. . . .

§ 125.241 Applicability.

This subpart prescribes rules, in addition to those prescribed in other parts of this chapter, for the maintenance of airplanes, airframes, aircraft engines, propellers, appliances, each item of survival and emergency equipment, and their component parts operated under this part.

§ 125.243 Certificate holder's responsibilities.

(a) With regard to airplanes, including airframes, aircraft engines, propellers, appliances, and survival and emergency equipment, operated by a certificate holder, that certificate holder is primarily responsible for—

(1) Airworthiness;

(2) The performance of maintenance, preventive maintenance, and alteration in accordance with applicable regulations and the certificate holder's manual;

(3) The scheduling and performance of inspections required by this part; and

(4) Ensuring that maintenance personnel make entries in the airplane maintenance log and maintenance records which meet the requirements of Part 43 of this chapter and the certificate holder's manual, and which indicate that the airplane has been approved for return to service after maintenance, preventive maintenance, or alteration has been performed.

Source: Code of Federal Regulations, Title 14, Chapter 1 (1-1-86 Edition), Federal Aviation Administration, Department of Transportation.

government does, from how it hires and fires employees to how the IRS deals with taxpayers. The volume of federal rules is massive; a complete set would easily fill a floor-to-ceiling bookcase. The 1986 collection of existing rules, called the *Code of Federal Regulations,* comprises 192 volumes including 16 volumes on agriculture alone, another 14 on internal revenue, and individual volumes on subjects as diverse as American Indians, the Panama Canal, wildlife, and fisheries. Subjects range from accountants (including rules for suspending them from government contracts) to zoning (including rules limiting the height of buildings in national recreation areas). The true size of federal regulations is hard to measure by any objective standard—but unquestionably these rules touch nearly every part of the life of every citizen.

The rules come in great, sometimes amazing, detail. For example, the code has twenty-two pages of rules on bicycle safety, complete with five pages of technical diagrams. On bicycle brakes, Title 16 of the *Code of Federal Regulations* (CFR), section 1512.5, subsection 5, states: "a force of less than 44.5 N (10 lbf.) shall cause the brake pads to contact the braking surface of the wheel when applied to the handlever at a point 25 mm (1.0 in.) from the open end of the handlebar." Other sections cover every other part of the bicycle in equal detail, and, as a result, bicycle manufacturers must meet a complicated set of standards. The federal government does not dispatch an army of inspectors to factories to examine the bicycles coming off the line. Instead, as in air safety, bicycle manufacturers must certify that they meet the federal government's standards by saying so on a "hang tag" attached to each bicycle. (The hang tag itself must meet the standards of Title 16, CFR, section 1512.19(d)(1).) Bicycle safety also relies on proxies: minimum safety standards defined by the federal government are administered by private-sector companies and backed up by private certifications and federal spot inspections.

Such rules are part of the "new" social regulation that developed in the 1960s and 1970s. Although the federal government since the 1800s had been involved in regulating social policy, these two decades witnessed a remarkable growth in federal regulation of health, safety, and equality. New agencies sprang up—for instance, the Occupational Safety and Health Administration, the Consumer Product Safety Commission, and the Environmental Protection Agency—to improve the safety of the workplace and of consumer goods and the quality of the air and water. At the same time, older agencies like the Food and Drug Administration took on new responsibilities for examining, for example, the cancer-causing properties of food additives. Safety regulations, in fact, enjoy broader public support than any other kind of federal rules. A 1987 *Wall Street Journal*/NBC News poll, in fact, revealed that 61 percent of those surveyed believed there should be more government regulation of the environment. Only 6 percent thought there should be less.[3]

The "old" economic regulation, by comparison, concentrated principally on the price, standards for service, and rules for entrance and exit from an industry. The Federal Communications Commission regulated the broadcast industry, the Interstate Commerce Commission interstate (but not intrastate) trucking, and the Civil Aeronautics Board the routes planes were allowed to fly and the fares they could charge. When the pace and scope of federal regulation exploded in the 1960s and 1970s, however, it was largely in the areas of social regulation. Old-style economic regulation, in fact, was receding even as new-style social regulation galloped forward. The deregulation of the airline industry in 1978, for example, meant the death of the Civil Aeronautics Board a few years later. Not until the Reagan administration was the regulatory pace dramatically slowed, however. In the 1980s adopting new regulations became more difficult because of new procedural requirements and budget cuts that reduced regulatory agency staffs. A 1987 survey showed that 38 percent of the American people believed there was too much government regulation of the economy, but even these results represent a swing toward regulation. In 1980 more than two-thirds of those surveyed believed the federal government had overregulated business and damaged the economy.[4]

Nearly every law passed by Congress requires federal agencies to write rules to implement it, and changing conditions, as well as judicial challenges and interest-group complaints, mean old rules have to be updated. Regulation is part of the very fiber of government action, both as a policy strategy in its own right (as in ensuring airline safety) or as a tool for implementing other policy strategies (such as tax expenditures or loan programs).

There are, in fact, at least four kinds of regulation. First is federal regulation of individuals. The tax code, for example, contains volumes of rules about how individuals must pay tax on their income. Second, there is federal regulation of organizations, especially of corporations. Not only does the corporate tax code influence a wide range of governmental actions, but federal rules also govern the conduct of many private-sector activities, such as banking.[5] Third is federal regulation of state and local governments. These governments, as we saw in Chapter 4, must comply with rules ranging from what to do with federal grant money to how to run sewage treatment facilities.[6] Fourth, the federal government regulates itself, with rules covering everything from per-

125

sonnel procedures to purchasing standards.

Regulation, in short, is an inevitable, universal phenomenon that everyone complains about but which no one can avoid. No program can operate without rules. And, when problems occur, from aircraft disasters to contract fraud, nearly everyone's reaction is, "The federal government should have a rule to prevent this."

Anatomy of the crash

That, indeed, was the public reaction after the Gander crash. Even though the charter was operated by the multinational peacekeeping force and not by the Pentagon, critics wondered how American military officials could trust the lives of soldiers to an airline flying, in the words of Captain Manion, "sleazy" equipment. Arrow Air was an American airline with an American crew operating under the FAA's safety regulations—and the crash killed American service personnel.

Military contract airlines

Arrow Air was a major Pentagon contractor, part of the military's Civil Air Reserve Fleet. This fleet dated from 1959, when Congress established a policy of relying as much as possible on civilian airlines to fly military personnel. In return for Pentagon contracts to fly troops around the world, airlines agreed to make their planes available to the military in case of national emergency. These airlines—twenty-four in all—ranged from United, Continental, and Pan Am to lesser known lines like Tower International, Evergreen International, and Arrow Air. Together they had 350 long-range planes committed to the air reserve fleet.

Congress was interested in minimizing federal investment in passenger aircraft and concentrating federal dollars instead on aircraft for the military's unique transport needs. The airlines were eager to sign up such lucrative business. It was a good deal for both sides: the military gained access to a large fleet of passenger aircraft and the airlines received large contracts. These contracts, in fact, move about 95 percent of all people and 30 percent of all cargo for the Department of Defense. In 1985 the Pentagon paid $1.15 billion for air charters, 3 percent of all revenue earned by American air carriers. The Pentagon, in fact, is the largest single customer of civilian airlines.[7]

Arrow Air had a longer history than many of the other contract airlines. Just after World War II chairman of the board George E. Batchelor began building the airline with two used DC-3s. Arrow Air halted operations in 1953 when the Civil Aeronautics Board, exercising old-style economic regulation, restricted the operations of many small carriers. Following airline deregulation in 1978 and the death of the CAB, however, Batchelor in 1981 brought Arrow Air back into business and expanded the airline's service to nearly 200 flights per week. Arrow Air earned military contracts to fly American armed forces around the world; the company did $33.6 million in business with the Pentagon in 1985 and received another $13.5 million contract for 1986. On both civilian and military business, its planes flew more than 1 million passengers to 245 cities around the world.[8]

For the safety of its soldiers, the Pentagon relied on Arrow Air's compliance with the FAA's rules. After the crash, however, investigators learned that the DC-8 that crashed in Gander had been involved in two previous incidents, both involving armed services personnel. In July, five months before the crash, the pilot had aborted a takeoff from Toledo, Ohio, when flames came out of one of the engines. Just a month before the crash, in November, another pilot was taking off from Grand Rapids, Michigan, to fly 126 military passengers to Camp Lejeune, North Carolina. The plane scraped and damaged its tail along the runway, and the pilot aborted the takeoff. The crew discovered that all of the passengers were sitting in the rear of the plane, throwing off the balance of the plane. The pilot had never checked the plane's seating. After redistributing the passengers he took off.

In neither case did the Arrow Air crews report the incidents to the FAA as regulations required. Neither did the crews enter the incidents in the plane's log, as the rules mandated. In fact, the pilot in the November incident did not even check the tail damage before taking off again. Investigators suspected that Arrow Air's crew behavior had been sloppy and that its maintenance had been deficient. A mechanic working under contract to Arrow in July and August before the crash, in fact, found the plane in such poor condition that he refused to sign the plane's log, the register of compliance with federal regulations. He discovered that he had to add excessive amounts of oil to one engine and that corrosive water was leaking from the toilet system into the plane's belly. The mechanic told the House Armed Services Committee that he never would have flown the plane.[9]

Maintenance problems

Nearly two years earlier, the FAA had been so concerned about maintenance problems in general that it launched unprecedented safety inspections of 327 airlines. Agency officials discovered that airlines with military contracts had almost twice as many serious problems as did airlines without contracts. Furthermore, these problems were concentrated among the small contract carriers. Arrow Air ranked ninth among all the airlines studied in the number of the most serious problems discovered—problems uncovered at a rate of 70 in every 100 inspections.[10]

The FAA included Arrow among 43 airlines identified for immediate follow-up inspections. Arrow Air, the FAA discovered, had a history of lengthy deferrals in maintenance and "weak recordkeeping." FAA inspectors reported, "Arrow could not produce a formal maintenance program" and its tool storage area was a "shambles." The FAA fined Arrow Air $34,000 for violating federal regulations. The airline grudgingly paid. "We settled without admitting guilt," Chairman Batchelor said. "Rather than fight it, it was cheaper to pay." [11]

Arrow Air officials maintained, furthermore, that they were operating a safe airline and that the Gander crash was an isolated, unfortunate accident. Richard P. Skully, senior vice-president for operations and maintenance, admitted to a subcommittee of the Senate Governmental Affairs Committee that Arrow had been guilty of "certain deficiencies" in recordkeeping. However, he said, Arrow was a fully certified air carrier that met the same FAA rules and conducted the same inspections as the major airlines. Meeting these standards, he contended, meant that Arrow was safe to fly. Batchelor, moreover, assured the senators that "there is only one way to do things when it comes to safety—the right way. We have never placed any limit on budgetary resources needed for maintenance." He concluded, "At no time did I or would I ask a pilot to fly an aircraft he believed to be unsafe." [12]

Former Arrow Air pilot Daniel E. Hood, though, sharply questioned the assurances that Skully and Batchelor had made. Hood, who had lost his fiancée, an Arrow Air flight attendant, in the crash, charged, "Arrow would use the Minimum Equipment List, which sets forth the minimum equipment required for certain flight conditions, as the maximum level for maintenance." The company, furthermore, deferred maintenance on so many items that safety was lowered. One Arrow Boeing 707, he told the senators, was nicknamed "pre-death" by the airline's pilots because of its recurring maintenance problems. "Arrow's periodic maintenance was also deficient," he said, and he explained with a story about a plane he had flown. The plane had lost all its hydraulic fluid and the landing gear would not work. The crew then tried to extend the landing gear manually but found it was stuck. He luckily was able to recover enough hydraulic pressure to bump the right landing gear out of the lock position before that fluid was lost overboard, and he nursed the plane to a safe landing. After the plane landed, mechanics discovered that the emergency landing gear components were "bent and corroded," which meant that "the emergency system had not been periodically checked as it should have been." He concluded that "when an emergency arose where the manual system was needed, the aircraft was not equipped to meet that emergency."

Hood also charged that Arrow pressured its pilots to fly more hours than FAA rules allowed. On several occasions, he testified, he informed the headquarters office that he would exceed the maximum hours if he continued to fly past a certain point. "When I arrived at the stopping place, no replacement was available and a planeload of passengers was waiting to go on. At that point, the dispatcher would tell me that if I did not continue to fly, Arrow's MAC [the Pentagon's Military Airlift Command] contracts would be cancelled and everyone at Arrow would lose their jobs." He concluded, "This type of pressure on pilots is intolerable." [13]

The FAA responded in January 1986 to such charges with "special accelerated inspections" of airlines with military contracts. The agency increased spot checks of the airlines by five times, to one in every two flights, to be conducted at stops on military bases. Secretary of Transportation Elizabeth Hanford Dole, whose department includes the FAA, said, "We want to assure ourselves and the public beyond a shadow of a doubt that these carriers are operating with the highest standards of safety." [14] The accident and subsequent news reports, however, seriously cut into Arrow Air's business. The Pentagon suspended Arrow from its military contracts and in February 1986 the airline filed for bankruptcy. The jobs of more than 400 employees were the final casualty of the crash.

Though investigators had a difficult time determining the actual cause of the accident, they suggested that the "probable primary cause" was the extra weight of snow on the wings that caused the plane to stall on takeoff. The physical evidence was so badly burned that the crash scene produced few clues, but computer simulations showed that the accident could not be replicated without the snow—and the failure to de-ice. Miscalculations by the crew on the weight of fuel and baggage on board might have contributed to the crash. So too might reduced power in one engine, a chronic maintenance problem on other planes flown by Arrow. In any event, the investigators concluded that the plane stalled during takeoff because of too much weight or too little power and then dived into the ground. The plane was also, they argued, in shabby condition. [15]

The tragedy in Gander thus had two significant effects. It intensified the debate over the quality of air safety in the years following airline deregulation. The crash also increased concern about a system that relies on the performance of government proxies for complying with safety regulations.

Regulation and air safety

In 1978 Civil Aeronautics Board chairman Alfred Kahn won a campaign to put his own agency out of business: to end the federal government's control over which airlines could serve which cities at which prices. Deregulation produced a veritable revolution in air travel. A host of new commuter airlines sprang up to serve smaller towns, in many places replacing larger airlines that pulled out of unprofitable smaller markets. Meanwhile, major new airlines like People's Express started new coast-to-coast and transatlantic service at fares a fraction of what other airlines used to charge. People's Express worked like no other airline. Passengers had to get used to no-frills service, to airline executives doubling as flight attendants or baggage handlers, and sometimes to massive over-booking, a practice that left passengers with confirmed reservations standing at the gate as full planes took off. (Such management problems, in fact, led to a major reorganization of the company in early 1987, when People's Express merged with Continental Airlines.)

All in all, in just a few years the airline industry went through the biggest changes in its entire history. The number of air carriers doubled, from 240 in 1978 to 500 in 1984. At the same time, budget cuts reduced the number of FAA safety inspectors from 2,100 in 1979 to more than 1,300 in 1984. The cuts also increased attrition, so by fiscal year 1988, the U.S. General Accounting Office estimated, 40 percent of all FAA inspectors would have fewer than three years of experience.[16]

Such changes, the staff of the House Armed Services Committee asserted, have "created a situation in which no one can assure the public with any degree of confidence that the airlines they are flying are truly safe," because "the FAA's ability to conduct inspections and monitor the safety of these airlines had diminished greatly." The staff concluded, "In a nutshell, airline safety has become a cost-accountable item in an airline system which now lives by an inescapable credo: cut costs to the bone wherever possible."[17]

While many defenders of the air industry might suggest that the House committee staff had dramatically exaggerated the extent of the problem, deregulation had certainly created new safety problems. There unquestionably is a difference, as the staff report pointed out, between mechanics working in the rain on an aging fleet of DC-8s, rarely used by scheduled airlines in the mid-1980s, and other mechanics working in a major airline's multimillion-dollar service hangars. The danger is that for financially pressed airlines, especially smaller charter lines, the FAA's minimum maintenance standards could become the effective maximum standards. The danger also is that FAA inspectors, stretched thin because of budget cuts and equipped with little experience because of turnover, would at the same time be less effective in policing airline maintenance. The ultimate danger is that the existing system of safety-by-proxy could break down under the financial pressures of a newly competitive air market.[18]

Especially after the Gander crash, the FAA was determined to put high priority on ensuring that airlines met the maintenance standards. It increased the number both of inspections and inspectors. In 1986, furthermore, the FAA levied huge fines against some of the nation's major airlines for violating the maintenance regulations. American Airlines paid a $1.5 million fine, while Pan Am paid an even larger $2 million fine. The FAA hit Eastern Airlines with a record $9.5 million judgment for an alleged 78,372 safety violations, one for each flight conducted with substandard equipment.

Some airline officials pointed out that safety in the industry was steadily improving and that in 1986 there was not a single fatality among the large American air carriers. Some critics wondered, however, if the safety record might be due more to good luck than compliance with the safety regulations. William Jackson, vice president of the Air Transport Association, the industry's trade group, acknowledged "Our emphasis on safe operations has given us an incredible skein of good luck." Many airline pilots, moreover, believed that their luck was running thin; a survey revealed that 43 percent of the pilots surveyed agreed that deregulation had adversely affected safety. One pilot, in fact, admitted he had flown his jet despite thirteen red tags hanging around the cockpit, each representing a part on which the airline had deferred needed maintenance.[19]

Thus, airline safety is built upon a complex system made up of federal rules that set the standards, airlines' investment in facilities and procedures to meet those standards, their recordkeeping demonstrating their compliance, and FAA inspectors keeping the airlines honest. In the end, though, the effectiveness of airline safety regulations depends most on the air carriers' acceptance of their role as proxies for federal air safety rules. As GAO associate director Herbert R. McClure argued, "The whole system is built on airlines voluntarily complying. If they don't keep their records up to date, there is no way the FAA can know if an airline is complying." [20]

Disagreements between the FAA and the airlines, though, are inevitable. There are differences in judgment about the level of maintenance actually required, about the benefits of maintenance and other safety issues weighed against their costs. In fact, conflicts between regulators and the regulated are a fact of life. The ultimate challenge of regulation thus is the task not only of making the rules work but, more fundamentally, of determining what the goal of the rules should be and how to balance each goal against competing ones.

Consensus on goals

The keystone of all government-by-proxy strategies—regulation no less than any other—is consensus on goals. Yet disagreement over goals is inevitable because conflict is an inherent feature of government by proxy. Consensus on goals—and therefore success in each policy—is thus more elusive with proxies than with direct administration of programs.

In government by proxy the federal government and its nonfederal proxies are partners. But the programs and the goals represent only a portion, often a small one, of each proxy's concerns. Pentagon contracts were an important but not the only part of Arrow Air's business. Similarly, tax policy is an important but not the only incentive for the behavior of individuals and corporations. Federal grants represent a large but not an exclusive source of state and local revenues. Thus, government by proxy is a somewhat unbalanced partnership. To a federal agency such as the FAA, administering a program for airline safety is the very core of its existence. However, the airline responsible for following the FAA's rules has other concerns that compete with the air safety program.

Successful policy implementation thus depends on two steps. First, the federal government and its proxies must reach at least rough consensus on goals. Second, the federal program's goals must mesh with the larger universe of each proxy's values. The second condition, of course, is often problematic, because other things may matter more to proxies than the federal goals. No airline, for example, would ever argue that safety is less important than other objectives, but every airline faces the hard choice of weighing expenditures for maintenance against other expenses and against the need to turn a profit.

Differences in goals—and problems in achieving program "success"—are thus the rule, not the exception, in government by proxy.

132

Each organization has its own rigidities, shaped by its own values, and efforts to change these characteristics will always court conflicts. The more actors from more groups and organizations that are involved in a policy, the greater the potential for conflict—and the greater the need for some way of bridging the gaps among the groups.[21] The federal government cannot regulate away disagreements or differences in values. This issue, in fact, lies at the core of most of the problems discussed in this book.

The policy-making process often is not well equipped to resolve these differences. In regulation, for example, the Administrative Procedure Act lays out a "formal rule making" process similar to a trial that creates a formal record of each side of the regulatory case. An administrative law judge then weighs the record and issues a formal regulatory decision; the accumulated weight of such decisions then becomes the body of regulations the regulated must follow. Formal rule making thus is very cumbersome, and agencies often use "informal rule making." They draft proposed regulations, publish them for comment, collect public reactions, and then revise the proposed regulation into a final rule.

Regulatory negotiation

The complexity of rule making belies these relatively straightforward procedures. Congress's tendency to express the standards in vague language (to reach compromise during the legislative process) inevitably creates disputes. Factual issues are often complex and thus subject to widely varying interpretations. Most regulations, furthermore, are not backed by a clear political consensus. In writing rules, therefore, a government agency typically must exercise substantial discretion—and, in doing so, it "can expect opposition to almost every rule it develops," as Lawrence Susskind and Gerald McMahon put it.[22]

Such pressures sometimes lead regulators to meet privately with affected parties to iron out differences before publishing the rules. Private deal making can settle some disputes, but at a high cost: other affected parties might not be notified of the meeting and thus find their legitimate interests not recognized in the final rule. Environmentalists were infuriated to learn that top EPA officials in the first Reagan administration had met privately over lunch with industry executives to discuss environmental rules. In 1983, for example, Congress investigated former EPA assistant adminstrator Rita M. Lavelle for political favoritism in regulating the cleanup of hazardous wastes. A federal jury later convicted her for lying about her ties to regulated industry. The environmentalists feared that such a back channel would make EPA more sympathetic to industry's views and that environmental interests would suffer. The result of such contacts is inevitably to increase the litigation over federal rules and to undermine confidence in the rule-making process.

In the mid-1970s some analysts began suggesting that the problem was principally one of resolving basic differences in values among those involved. The Administrative Conference of the United States in 1982 recommended that federal agencies experiment with a new, negotiated approach to rule making. "Experience indicates that if the parties in interest were to work together to negotiate the text of a proposed rule," the conference argued, they might be able to write a better rule "that is acceptable to the respective interests, all within the contours" of the legislation. The premise was that "rulemaking, through negotiation, will result in an improved process and better rules."[23]

Regulatory negotiation was especially attractive to William D. Ruckelshaus, the first administrator of the Environmental Protection Agency (EPA), who had been brought back to rebuild the agency's tarnished reputation after the tenure of Anne Gorsuch Burford. The battles over EPA rules, he said, hurt everyone. Constant litigation had cost enormous sums of money and denied business "the predictability it needs to make wise investment decisions." For environmental groups, litigation meant long delays in enforcing the standards for which they had fought.[24] At EPA, in fact, 80 percent of the 300 regulations proposed each year were ending up in court, and EPA was devoting about 125 staff-years (the equivalent of 125 persons working full time) to regulatory litigation. Such litigation significantly changed 30 percent of EPA's rules.[25] The result, said Ruckelshaus's successor, Lee M. Thomas, was that such disputes "will ultimately bog our cleanup effort down in a quagmire of litigation and further delay."[26]

In negotiated rule making, the agency would bring all of the affected parties together in a series of sessions to work out a mutually acceptable rule. By bargaining out a regulation everyone could live with, EPA officials hoped to broaden support for the rule and thereby to avoid challenges in court. As Thomas put it, "I am confident we can come up with better rules that we can implement rather than litigate." The goal was to develop "a better rule, arrived at by listening to and talking with those more directly affected by it."[27]

The major advantage was to change the rules of the game from litigation to problem solving. As EPA's assistant administrator, Milton Russell, explained, the process was useful "because it gets us out of win-lose situations when sometimes win-win situations are possible." [28] Furthermore, another important benefit was bringing contacts between regulators and the regulated out into the open. Secret negotiating sessions had been commonplace throughout the federal government. Regulatory negotiation was a way to bring such sessions into the sunlight, to resolve conflicts before the regulations were published (and thus avoid litigation) but to do so in a way that would not give one party an advantage over any other.

Pesticide exemptions

In 1972 Congress passed the Federal Insecticide, Fungicide, and Rodenticide Act, which gave EPA strong powers to control pesticides. [29] Manufacturers wanting to market new pesticides first had to document any risks the chemicals posed to human health. However, data about the dangers of the chemicals were often not available, and full testing could take up to four years. Both manufacturers, who wanted to start selling the product, and users, who wanted to put it to work, found the long delay unacceptable.

The law gave EPA the right to grant exemptions in case of emergency needs. The obvious problem, however, was defining what constituted an emergency. The great danger was that EPA might use its discretion to favor some manufacturers over others in granting exemptions. Even in routine situations, the demand for exemptions was enormous. From just 1978 to 1982, for example, the number of emergency exemptions increased from 199 to 724. To make matters worse, the rules setting out how manufacturers should apply for the exemptions were difficult to read and also vague about how EPA should weigh each request. Critics wondered, in fact, if EPA considered the risks at all in granting so many exemptions, and Congress worried that industries or state governments might be using the exemptions to get around the act's tough requirements.

EPA could have used traditional rule-making procedures to draft new rules on exemptions, but instead agency officials in April 1985 decided to use the regulatory negotiation process. In particular, EPA wanted to determine how long the emergency exemptions ought to last once granted. If the exemptions were too long, manufacturers could more easily avoid the act's requirements; if they were too short, there would be repeated requests for extensions. EPA, in addition, had to define more precisely what an "emergency" was and what information an industry should provide.

EPA officials appointed LaJuana Wilcher as the "facilitator," to conduct the negotiations and to serve as an "honest broker." Wilcher was from EPA's general counsel's office and had not previously been directly involved in making, administering, or enforcing the rule, and thus could ensure that EPA's legislative responsibilities were met without being influenced by past EPA activities in the area. The agency then assembled a group of twenty-two interested parties, including environmental groups (such as the National Audubon Society); state organizations with the responsibility for administering the regulations (such as the Association of American Pesticide Control Officials); pesticide users (such as the American Farm Bureau Association); and manufacturers and processors (such as the National Food Processors Association).

Before beginning the process, EPA set a four-month deadline for producing an agreement; if participants could not reach a consensus by then, the agency would stop the proceedings and write rules on its own. Some change in regulations was inevitable, so all of the participants had a stake in making sure their voices were heard. Members of the committee, however, had very different views. Environmentalists, of course, favored relatively tight rules, while agricultural interests pressed for looser standards. Even among participants from the same groups, however, there were often wide differences in perspective, depending on the region of the country and the kind of crops involved.

The committee met on September 28, 1984, and began working. Everyone agreed to be bound by a formal document to be produced at the end. Everyone was aiming at a single target, one whose meaning would be clear. The committee divided into three working groups: one to define "emergency," a second to discuss health and safety issues, and the third to resolve implementation problems. In the early stages, the members spent most of their time collecting facts, but as the deadline approached the participants spent much more time staking out their positions. During the final two-day session the group hammered out an agreement and on January 16, 1985, the participants signed their recommendation.

EPA published the agreement as a proposed regulation three months later. During the comment period, the agency received only nineteen reactions, contrasting with the hundreds of comments that usually followed proposed regulations. Three of these comments, furthermore, were from participants in the process supporting the results, and the rest raised relatively minor issues. EPA officials collected all of the comments and circulated them among the participants, who decided to stick with the draft they had originally signed. Several months later, EPA officially issued the regulation, in far less time than rule making usually required—and without the predictable flood of court challenges.

Prospects and problems

Negotiated rule making is not for every agency or for every problem. It requires credible spokespersons for the key interests involved and a nonpartisan mediator to help move the group toward consensus. The groups, furthermore, cannot be too large; negotiating sessions of about twenty to twenty-five participants seem to work best. Successful negotiations require that the regulatory dispute be "ripe" and ready for solution, with the issues neither too embryonic (and hence too unformed) nor too far advanced (with the sides too hardened). Experts on negotiation argue that the issue should not be too technically complex. Neither should it be too large (thus making any side hesitant to compromise) nor too minor (making the substantial investment in the negotiating sessions not worthwhile).[30]

Needless to say, negotiated rule making is not an easy path. Some parties may believe they stand a better chance of nudging the regulation their way by taking the issue to court or exerting pressure behind the scenes. The process, furthermore, is extremely expensive. Kelly M. Brown, manager of emission control planning for the Ford Motor Company, said that in one EPA negotiated rule making, "My travel budget got destroyed." Furthermore, as David Doniger, a staff attorney for the National Resources Defense Council, explained, "To participate in a regulatory negotiation takes about ten times as much of our resources as commenting on a rule" in the more typical informal rule-making process.[31]

Still, EPA has found the process valuable, most of all because it offers the chance for disputing parties to gain what EPA administrator Thomas called "ownership" in the final rule: by working with the other parties to find common ground, the participants are more likely to be committed to the result and less likely to challenge it in court. "Consultation may produce a better rule, and keep us out of court at the same time," Thomas said.[32] Even with the costs and problems, moreover, past participants in negotiation sessions tend to become advocates of the process.[33] Negotiation offers an intriguing solution to the most troublesome problem of government by proxy: bridging the gap between the goals of government and its proxies through bargaining.

However, such bargaining raises even more fundamental issues. Regulators act under delegation of authority from Congress to implement the laws that Congress adopts. They are legally bound to follow those laws, even if that leads to litigation. Winning public support is not their main purpose. Federal officials could easily avoid disputes and conflicts simply by caving in to the wishes of interest groups, but that obviously is not in the public interest. The "nondelegation doctrine" means that those to whom Congress has delegated responsibility cannot delegate it further. Allowing interested parties to sit around a table and shape a regulation directly affecting them further complicates the constitutional issue: how can an agency negotiate a new rule with interested parties without surrendering decision-making power to them, in violation of the nondelegation doctrine? Supporters of the process, however, point out that conversations between regulators and the regulated are inevitable in the politics of any level of government. The regulatory negotiation process ensures that those conversations take place in the open, with all interested parties represented. Secrecy in communication is the only big loser.

EPA officials are keenly aware of their responsibility to follow congressional intent, and they are constantly alert to their own professional standards. "I think we are first among equals," explained Chris Kirtz, director of EPA's regulatory negotiation project. Furthermore, the agency makes a concerted effort to include the affected parties in the negotiations. If the resources available to the different parties are unequal—as they undoubtedly would be in disputes between large corporations and small public-interest environmental groups—EPA administers a fund to pay for travel and short-time consulting for participants who otherwise could not afford it.[34] Still, negotiation is a delicate balancing act: on one hand, it involves finding agreement among the parties that satisfies EPA's view of Congress's intent; and on the other hand, it must avoid giving tacit rule-making authority to interest groups.

Regulation thus presents a difficult government-by-proxy strategy. Instead of directly controlling the safety of airplanes or pesticides, the government shares responsibility with its proxies by establishing standards that private interests must follow. Ensuring compliance with these rules, however, is a difficult process. The government uses many verification procedures, such as log-keeping requirements and spot inspections, but in the end the performance of the regulatory system depends on the competence and good faith of millions of private citizens and organizations. What those standards should be, moreover, is typically the subject of lively debate. Regulators assume that the regulated will, as a matter of course, challenge *any* rule in court. In some cases, the federal government has reduced this problem by sharing responsibility with the regulated for deciding what the regulations should say. Regulatory negotiation short-circuits litigation, but it emphasizes the basic problem: how to reconcile the inevitable value conflicts of government by proxy while keeping the public interest paramount.

Conflicts of values _____

Within the complex relationships of government by proxy, the most fundamental—and inevitable—problem is meshing the values of government and its proxies. Any marriage is a matter of finding common ground among individuals while accommodating their differences. That can be hard enough between a man and a woman who love each other. It is far more difficult between two large organizations, and the responsibility of government officials to promote the public interest makes the task even more complex in government by proxy.

Government officials may be tempted to reduce value conflicts by bargaining differences away. The danger in this, however, is "the concept that implementation is its own reward," as Majone and Wildavsky explain it.[35] "Success" is more than lowered conflict, fewer delays, or a decrease in horror stories in the media. Less conflict does not necessarily mean that the goals of the legislation, as framed by Congress and the president, will be served. The very concept of "the public interest" is, of course, nebulous—notoriously difficult to define and quite naturally hard to judge. But this much is clear: in government programs the federal government's fundamental goals are paramount and cannot be negotiated away; and in government by proxy, the proxies are agents of federal goals, not simply of their own interests.

Bargaining can reduce political conflict and thus improve the chances for success in public policy. Government programs, however, do not exist simply to resolve the conflicts they create. There is a broader public purpose, however difficult to define, for which public policies were created. Success thus inevitably goes beyond negotiating away conflict. It depends on finding some way of resolving the basic dilemmas: bridging the gap in values between the government and its proxies, and ensuring that the legitimate goals of public programs—the public interest—always remain paramount and are not compromised.

Notes _____

1. *New York Times*, December 13, 1985, A14.
2. *New York Times*, December 17, 1985, B8.
3. Seymour Martin Lipset and William Schneider, *The Confidence Gap* (New York: Free Press, 1983), 241; *Wall Street Journal*, April 2, 1987, 1.
4. See Kenneth J. Meier, *Regulation* (New York: St. Martin's Press, 1985), 2-3; *Wall Street Journal*, April 2, 1987, 1.

5. Marver H. Bernstein, *Regulating Business by Independent Commission* (Princeton: Princeton University Press, 1955).

6. See Donald F. Kettl, *The Regulation of American Federalism* (Baton Rouge: Louisiana State University Press, 1983).

7. U.S. Congress, House of Representatives, Committee on Armed Services, *Report on the Safety of Aircraft Under Charter to the Department of Defense*, report, 99th Cong., 2d sess., 1986, 3-6.

8. *New York Times*, December 15, 1985, Sec. 1, 21; December 24, 1985, A9.

9. House Armed Services Committee, *Report on the Safety of Aircraft*, 13.

10. Ibid., 9.

11. *New York Times*, December 24, 1985, A9.

12. U.S. Congress, Senate, Committee on Governmental Affairs, Subcommittee on Permanent Investigations, hearings transcript, 1986.

13. Ibid.

14. *New York Times*, January 15, 1986, A13.

15. *Washington Post*, December 5, 1986, A21.

16. House Armed Services Committee, *Report on the Safety of Aircraft*, 7; *Washington Post*, May 16, 1986, A1.

17. House Armed Services Committee, *Report on the Safety of Aircraft*, 7.

18. Ibid.

19. *Time*, January 12, 1987, 26-27, 31.

20. *Washington Post*, May 16, 1986, A18.

21. See Herbert Kaufman, *The Limits of Organizational Change* (University, Ala.: University of Alabama Press, 1971), 72-75; James D. Thompson, *Organizations in Action* (New York: McGraw-Hill, 1967), 138-143; and Daniel Katz and Robert L. Kahn, *The Social Psychology of Organizations* (New York: John Wiley, 1966), 260-265.

22. Lawrence Susskind and Gerald McMahon, "The Theory and Practice of Negotiated Rulemaking," *Yale Journal on Regulation* 3 (1985): 135.

23. 1 CFR Sec. 305.82-84. See also ibid.; Philip J. Harter, "Negotiating Regulations: A Cure for Malaise," *Georgetown Law Journal* 71 (October 1982): 1-118; Henry H. Perritt, Jr., "Negotiated Rulemaking in Practice," *Journal of Policy Analysis and Management* 5 (Spring 1986): 482-495.

24. William D. Ruckelshaus, speech to Second National Conference on Environmental Dispute Resolution, Washington, D.C., October 1, 1984.

25. *National Journal*, November 15, 1986, 2764; Lee M. Thomas, speech to Third National Conference on Dispute Resolution, Washington, D.C., May 29, 1986; Susskind and McMahon, "The Theory and Practice of Negotiated Rulemaking," 134.

26. Lee M. Thomas, speech to National Academy of Public Administration, Spring Meeting, Washington, D.C., June 6, 1986.

27. Ibid.

28. *National Journal*, November 15, 1986, 2764-2765.

29. See Susskind and McMahon, "The Theory and Practice of Negotiated Rulemaking," 146-150; Harter, "Negotiating Regulations," 100-106.

30. *National Journal*, November 15, 1986, 2767; Daniel J. Fiorino and Chris Kirtz, "Breaking Down Walls: Negotiated Rulemaking at EPA," *Temple Environmental Law and Technical Journal* 4 (1985), 40; Philip J. Harter, "Dispute Resolution and Administrative Law: The History, Needs, and Future of a Complex Relationship," *Villanova Law Review* 29 (1983-1984): 1405-1406; Susskind and

McMahon, "The Theory and Practice of Negotiated Rulemaking"; and National Institute for Dispute Resolution, Washington, D.C., *Forum*, 1986.

31. Dispute Resolution, *Forum*, 9.
32. Thomas, speech, May 29, 1986.
33. Susskind and McMahon, "The Theory and Practice of Negotiated Rulemaking," 163.
34. Interview with the author, January 16, 1987.
35. Giandomenico Majone and Aaron Wildavsky, "Implementation as Evolution," in *Implementation*, 3d ed., ed Jeffrey L. Pressman and Aaron Wildavsky (Berkeley: University of California Press, 1984), 167.

Managing for success 7

Few events of recent history shook America as did the tragic end of the space shuttle *Challenger* on January 28, 1986. When the shuttle lifted off into the clear blue Florida sky that morning, the television networks captured a terrifying explosion of orange flame as the shuttle shattered into thousands of pieces. Over the next several days Americans watched videotaped replays of the disintegration of the spacecraft and the looks of horror on the faces of the crew's families. Because the shuttle in many ways symbolized the triumph of American technology over an alien environment, the disaster weakened the national self-confidence.

The Challenger investigation

An investigating commission appointed by President Ronald Reagan and headed by former secretary of state William P. Rogers discovered that the explosion resulted from the failure of a joint in the shuttle's solid rocket booster.[1] The booster, one of two solid-fuel rockets designed to send the shuttle into orbit, was made of several pieces laid end to end. Only 0.678 seconds after the rockets were ignited, the commission found, one of the joints developed a problem: the rocket's hot gases blew past putty and two rubber O-rings intended to seal the joints. By 57.788 seconds into the flight, a flame erupted from the joint and within seconds grew into a blowtorch focused on the shuttle's external fuel tank, full of liquid hydrogen and oxygen. Few combinations could have

143

been more explosive. At 73 seconds, the entire vehicle began to disintegrate and debris showered onto the ocean below. Investigators concluded that the crew never had a chance.

On closer examination, the investigators discovered that the disaster was not caused by an isolated mishap but by many accumulated problems. It was, the Rogers Commission reported, "an accident rooted in history." [2] The problems that led to the disaster illustrate the interconnected and enduring issues of government by proxy: getting accurate feedback from those running the programs and reconciling the goals of government and its proxies.

Information distortion

The night before the launch NASA officials at Marshall Space Flight Center, the command center for the propulsion system, debated for several hours with engineers and managers at Morton Thiokol, the contractor that built the rockets. Thiokol engineers worried that the cold weather predicted for Cape Canaveral the next morning would cause the O-rings to stiffen so that the joints would not seal properly. In fact, O-rings had at least partially failed in each of the previous shuttle launches made at temperatures below 61 degrees, and no shuttle had been launched at a temperature below 53 degrees.[3] Weather forecasters at the cape were predicting a hard freeze overnight with temperatures 30 degrees colder than that minimum. Knowing that the lower the temperature the worse the problem became, Thiokol's engineers concluded that "we should not fly outside of our data base, which was 53 degrees." [4] The practical effect of their recommendation was to postpone the next morning's scheduled flight.

To NASA officials that was an uncomfortable prospect. The shuttle had originally been scheduled for launch on January 22. Twice it was postponed because the equipment was not ready and another time because the weather was unacceptable. A fourth time, on January 27, the crew climbed on board, but launch-pad workers were unable to close the hatch because a wrench would not work properly. By the time they succeeded, the winds were too high and the launch had to be postponed again. NASA was anxious to get the shuttle off the ground, since each day's slippage in the schedule hurt not only the *Challenger* mission but all of the flights scheduled to follow it. Newspaper and television reporters had already made jokes at NASA's expense about the shuttle's continuing difficulties. Because of the damage already done to the agency's image, NASA wanted to avoid another day's delay.

NASA officials challenged Thiokol's engineers to prove that a launch in such cold weather would be dangerous. As Thiokol engineer Roger Boisjoly explained, it was a meeting "where the determination [from NASA] was to launch, and it was up to us to prove beyond a shadow of a doubt that it was not safe to do so. This is in total reverse to what the position usually is," with the burden of proof resting on those arguing it was safe to launch.[5] NASA's solid rocket booster manager, Lawrence Mulloy, refused to accept the engineers' arguments. "My God, Thiokol, when do you want me to launch, next April?" he is reported to have said. Marshall Space Flight Center deputy director George Hardy added, "I'm appalled at your recommendation."[6]

The haggling continued for hours. Thiokol engineer Allan McDonald challenged Mulloy's position and asked for a delay so NASA could consider the cold weather's effects on the rocket's performance. If anything happened, he told NASA officials, he would not want to have to explain the decision to a board of inquiry. McDonald was told that the problem was not his concern and that his worries would be passed along to higher officials. Thiokol's executives—not its engineers—finally caved in. While admitting to the engineers' concerns about the temperature, the executives signed a form recommending the launch. Mulloy passed along the clearance—but not the concerns—and the next morning the very catastrophe that McDonald and the Thiokol engineers had feared did occur. Within minutes after the accident most Thiokol engineers had guessed what had happened.

The Rogers Commission concluded that the reservations expressed that night by Thiokol's engineers were not adequately communicated to key NASA decision makers. The O-rings used to seal the rocket's joints, furthermore, had been under discussion for a long time, and the commission concluded that Marshall managers had not properly passed along the degree of concern that the engineers felt. The O-rings had been designated a "launch constraint" rated "criticality 1," meaning that if they failed the crew and craft would be lost. On each of six subsequent flights, however, Mulloy granted a waiver to allow the shuttle to continue to fly. Neither fact, the commission noted, was adequately communicated to the top two levels of NASA's launch review teams.[7]

Although information was passed along, its seriousness was not. Organizational theorists call this a form of "distortion"—either not forwarding bad news or disguising its severity. Theorists have long argued that the structure of bureaucracy impedes the flow of information. In a hierarchy, lower level employees must condense all information flowing up to top management, often emphasizing the good news and hiding the bad.[8] "The object," Charles Peters writes of some bureaucrats' motivations, "is to prevent information, particularly of an unpleasant character, from rising to the top of the agency, where it may produce results unpleasant to the lower ranks." [9]

The Rogers Commission was "troubled by what appears to be a propensity of management at Marshall to contain potentially serious problems rather than communicate them forward." The commission concluded that "there was a serious flaw in the decision making process leading up to the launch." [10] Low-level engineers, for example, rated the odds of a catastrophic failure of the solid-fuel rockets at 1 in 100. Top managers insisted instead that the odds were 1 in 100,000. That discrepancy, commission member and Nobel Prize-winning physicist Richard Feynman concluded, illustrated "an incredible lack of communication." [11]

NASA's communication breakdown went beyond the O-ring problem. Often, managers simply faced too much information. In its own report on the *Challenger* disaster, the House Committee on Science and Technology argued, "The existing communication system is disseminating too much information, often with little or no discrimination in its importance. Accordingly recipients often have difficulty 'separating the wheat from the chaff.' " [12] Furthermore, the number of NASA officials monitoring the quality and reliability of work done for the agency had decreased 71 percent since the mid-1970s, twice the level of reductions in the agency overall. At Marshall, the cuts were even greater, from 615 to 88 officials, a decrease of 86 percent. [13]

As a result, NASA was unable to monitor adequately the contracts that accounted for 85 percent of the agency's $7.5 billion annual budget. Auditors found that NASA often allowed contractors to finish work before agreeing on a price. Rockwell International Corporation spent $20 million on a propulsion system before it negotiated a price with NASA. Although the agency had expected to pay only $3.2 million, NASA paid the whole bill, because Rockwell had spent the money for the project. According to a former NASA contract monitor, the "cozy relationship" of the agency and its contractors made discovery of problems extremely difficult. [14]

Distortion presented another dilemma for NASA. The shuttle program, along with the agency's other programs, produced a huge volume of information. Lower level officials had to boil down the data or risk overwhelming top managers. Yet if they failed to pass key pieces of information up to managers, or if they did not emphasize its importance, managers could not choose the proper course. Top NASA officials, in fact, were fully briefed about difficulties with the O-rings, "but always in a way that didn't communicate the seriousness of the problem," according to the House committee report. NASA associate administrator for space flight, Jesse W. Moore, acknowledged that he was told about the problem on August 19, 1985—five months before the disaster—but added, "I believe there should have been a much stronger statement made to me that we have a much more serious problem." [15]

Distortion of information is an inevitable and serious problem. The predicament of having too much information or too little of the right information comes with a program of any complexity and with a bureaucracy of any size. Government by proxy aggravates the distortion. Passing needed information up the chain of command within a bureaucracy is a demanding task made even more difficult when a government bureaucracy first must acquire the information from an outside organization. Gung-ho contractors or state and local grantees are likely to suppress bad news. Cautious contractors eager to minimize their risks may not give any news at all. Poor performance—or outright fraud—can induce other contractors to conceal their guilt.

Furthermore, for regulations, loan programs, and tax expenditures, where the definition of "performance" is more elusive and the measurement of results more difficult, feedback is even harder to obtain. These programs work principally by altering the incentives of millions of industries or citizens. Good information on the effects—and even the costs—of these programs often emerges only slowly and tentatively.

The goals of different organizations naturally make them protective of their operations. The predictable reluctance of proxies to divulge information that reflects poorly on their activities magnifies the difficulty of getting good feedback.[16]

Goal conflicts

Another problem experienced by the shuttle program was the difficulty of reconciling the different goals of NASA and Thiokol. Organizations tend to deal with such differences by seeking certainty in the short term and flexibility in the long term. This obvious contradiction, as the case studies of earlier chapters as well as the NASA case illustrate, tends to be resolved in favor of the short run, with a bias toward certainty.[17] Dealing with immediate threats drives out long-range worries and creates a strong incentive to seek calm waters. The strong preference for short-term certainty also drives out planning for long-term problems. These problems, of course, eventually surface, often with catastrophic results.

Thiokol's short-run worries centered on its contract with NASA to supply the solid-fuel boosters. As a result of a competition more than a decade earlier, the contractor became NASA's sole supplier, and Congress was pressuring the agency to find a second source. Other potential contractors were themselves pressuring Congress for a share of the lucrative contract. Former senator Slade Gorton (R-Wash.), then chairman of the Senate Subcommittee for Science, Technology, and Space, speculated that the prospect of losing the contract "put some pressure on Thiokol's management the night before the launch." He concluded, "They must have felt that unless they went along with NASA and approved a launch, NASA would find another contractor that gives it answers it liked." [18]

In fact, the House investigation into the disaster argued, Thiokol's contract provided "far greater incentives to the contractor for minimizing costs and meeting schedules than for features related to safety and performance." [19] The Rogers Commission concluded that Thiokol "reversed its position" and recommended launch of the *Challenger* "in order to accommodate a major customer," NASA. [20] Thiokol managers were reluctant to jeopardize the NASA contract, especially given the pressures on NASA to find a second supplier. The bias toward certainty helped override the engineers' concerns about the cold weather.

NASA faced different pressures. Its budget was under attack as part of the overall reduction in government programs during the Reagan administration. Public support was waning; the news media pictured each cancellation as a new trial for a ne'er-do-well agency. Meanwhile, NASA was trying to make the shuttle "operational," changing it from an experimental system to a space truck scheduled for twice-monthly missions. As President Reagan put it on July 4, 1982, "The first priority of the STS [shuttle] program is to make the system fully operational and cost-effective in providing routine access to space." Attempts to meet such an ambitious schedule, however, "brought a number of difficulties, including the compression of training schedules, the lack of spare parts, and the focusing of resources on near-term problems," as the Rogers Commission noted. [21]

"You've got to think it [the disaster] had everything to do with the shuttle going 'operational,' " said one Rogers Commission investigator. In subtle ways, NASA "conveyed the thought that it didn't want to hear about delays" that would further annoy a Congress already questioning NASA's slipping schedule. The House committee agreed, finding "that NASA's drive to achieve a launch schedule of 24 flights per year created pressure throughout the agency that directly contributed to unsafe launch operations." The emphasis on the schedule "caused a realignment of priorities in the direction of productivity at the cost of safety," the committee concluded. [22]

For NASA, the bias toward short-term issues and certainty meant a sharp focus on keeping the shuttle's ambitious launch schedule to try to protect the agency's budget. The *New York Times* headlined the problem, "How See-No-Evil Doomed *Challenger.*" As commission member and Air Force general Donald J. Kutyna put it, "No one wanted to be the one who raised a show-stopping problem. No one had the guts to stand up and say, 'This thing is falling apart.' " [23] The result was the catastrophe that darkened Florida's sky on that January morning.

When any two organizations must cooperatively interact, feedback and goal problems are inevitable. These problems, coupled with a bias toward certainty and the short term, prevented NASA and Thiokol individually from diagnosing and solving the O-ring problem in time. The interaction of the two organizations, each with its own perspective and pressures, only worsened the problems. The lesson, thus, is clear, not only for the management of NASA but more broadly for the administration of government by proxy as well: the issues of feedback and goals are crucial ones that must be successfully resolved if the programs are to succeed.

Inevitable failures?

For cynics, the accident was yet another demonstration of the difficulty of running government programs well. In fact, an overwhelming sense of failure pervades the study of implementation, the administration of government programs. Scholars have suggested that most government programs never achieve what is expected of them.[24] Echoing the arguments of the public-choice school, Eugene Bardach tersely contends, "Government *ought* not to do many of the things liberal reform has traditionally asked of it; and even when, in some abstract sense, government does pursue appropriate goals, it is not well suited to achieving them." [25] Indeed, since the first major work on implementation, in which Jeffrey L. Pressman and Aaron Wildavsky sought to "build morals on a foundation of ruined hopes," implementation studies have been the province of pathologists: analysts who seek to explain why programs die.[26]

The result, among many citizens and perhaps even more among scholars, is a pervasive sense of dread about the administration of government programs, a sense that programs are doomed to fail. Things, of course, often do go wrong, and we have developed a treatment for the disease: stronger control, more leverage for government officials. Control, however, is an ill-fated managerial approach to government by proxy.

149

According to some analysts, programs often fail because policy makers cannot control the implementers. Richard E. Neustadt tells a classic story about the problem of control. He wrote that Harry S Truman joked about president-elect Dwight D. Eisenhower: "He'll sit here," Truman said, "and he'll say, Do this! Do that! *And nothing will happen.* Poor Ike—it won't be a bit like the Army. He'll find it very frustrating." [27] The story is telling because it reflects the typical approach to management, based on authority and control: decision makers choose goals, develop plans to meet those goals, transmit plans to the bureaucracy, and then supply resources and incentives to allow the bureaucracy to perform. This approach also guides the classical theory of hierarchy, which explains that government authority flows from the decision maker at the top to the bureaucrat at the bottom who is responsible for executing the policy. According to the theory, programs work best with this chain of authority. Each person in the hierarchy has specialized skills to perform part of the task.

Although such tight control is obviously impossible, as Truman's warning to Eisenhower shows, this model is still a staple of management theory. With the growth of government by proxy, though, control through hierarchy is unworkable even in theory, because policy makers do not control those outside the bureaucracy who eventually carry out their decisions. Government by proxy is essentially a strategy of decentralization, of transferring key decisions down—and out of—the federal bureaucracy into the hands of third parties.

Nevertheless, when problems threaten and failures occur, the usual approach is to try to recapture control through two recurring patterns: the regulation-recentralization reflex and the "unleashing-the-auditors" reflex.

The regulation-recentralization reflex

The usual response to struggling or failing programs is to write rules and regulations to make sure that the problems never recur, and to draw power back to the center to make sure that the rules stick. Some rules, of course, are patently ridiculous, but they rarely emerge from stupidity or malice. Instead, as research into individual cases reveals, every rule, no matter how ridiculous, exists to prevent the repetition of some problem in the past.

The horror-story syndrome. This decentralization-recentralization pattern has typically been the product of two syndromes, as pointed out by R. James Woolsey, a member of the Packard Commission, President Reagan's commission investigating the Pentagon.[28] One is the *horror-story syndrome,* in which highly visible problems arising from a decentralized program prompt calls for recentralization. For instance, critics have seen the failure of the Divad as evidence that the urge to decentralize is misguided. Troubled programs then are recentralized to reassert federal control, and rules are written to guarantee that the problems are not repeated.

In the Community Development program, publicity about uses of grants—for instance, for planting trees on a road leading to a country club—brought new rules limiting local discretion. The Packard Commission on defense management concluded that the widely publicized defense procurement problems were due in large part to inadequate central control of the process. To recapture control, the commission argued for a new central procurement czar, an under secretary of defense for acquisition.[29]

The casework syndrome. Another source of the regulation-recentralization reflex is the *casework syndrome.* Whether grilled at congressional committee hearings or pressured by presidential agents, federal administrators often find themselves responsible for explaining the individual decisions of far-off service producers outside the federal bureaucracy. In the Community Development program, for example, members of Congress quizzed top officials from the Department of Housing and Urban Development about minute details in the local governments' applications. With thousands of communities participating in the program, these officials could not reasonably control each item on each application, but members of Congress nevertheless held them responsible.[30] Defense program managers also find themselves called before congressional committees to answer for the behavior of individual contractors among the thousands doing defense work. Administrators of the federal Guaranteed Student Loan program must explain the high rate of defaults.

Regulation and recentralization. The administrator's reflex is defensive: recentralizing and writing new rules to prevent problems from recurring. After the *Challenger* exploded, for example, the investigating commission found that too much power was in the hands of contractors and NASA's program managers in individual "centers," the decentralized groups that manage individual shuttle components. The commission's report argued, "The project managers for the various elements of the shuttle program felt more accountable to their center management than to the shuttle program organization." The centers had become too independent of the agency's managers.[31]

The *Challenger* disaster demonstrated that the regulation-recentralization reflex is sometimes justified. More often, however, this reaction is the product of an intolerance for error. Because of the political costs of adverse publicity, especially the erosion of public support, managers often feel obliged to avoid the repetition of problems at all costs. Managers in this difficult position maintain public support by demonstrating that they are taking aggressive, corrective action, such as writing new rules or recentralizing parts of the program.

Centralization, though, often breeds its own problems. California, for example, centralized the responsibility for most human services into one large state agency. The goal was to improve coordination and management of services, to ensure that people requiring a combination of services did not fall through the cracks. However, as Brian O'Connell, president of Independent Sector, a Washington-based interest group representing nonprofit organizations, has pointed out, "The problem was that the cracks became chasms. The department was so large and was so far removed from Eureka or San Diego that it was totally efficient but grossly expensive. Because of its size and distance, it was completely insensitive to the people it was designed to serve, and it was even inaccessible to their elected representatives." [32]

This reflex, furthermore, can have a pernicious effect on the administrators themselves. Working in an agency under attack can erode morale, increase turnover, and make administrators less responsive and more remote. Recentralization, moreover, can increase the layers of an agency and thus the distance between any administrator and the front lines of service delivery. That, in turn, can make it harder to recruit and keep good administrators. What makes government work exciting is the feeling that an administrator can make a policy difference. When too many layers of bureaucracy pile up, the rewards diminish.

The point is not that either centralization or decentralization is superior. A generation of research in public administration has demonstrated that each has its advantages in different circumstances. [33] Rather, the argument is that the blind retreat to strategies of control—regulation and recentralization—to cure the defects of decentralization often only breeds more problems. Programs can become less responsive to the citizens they were designed to serve as the distance from managers to those citizens increases. Programs can become less flexible and less effective as administrators become disabled by rules and crosscutting restraints. Furthermore, administrators can find themselves tied to regulations based on the least common denominator: rules designed to prevent any problem, no matter how rare. The response to problems of a few thus become the regulatory burdens of many. While recentralization and regulation are sometimes necessary responses to the problems of decentralized, third-party programs, they tend to be adopted blindly in a pathological reflex to problems, a reflex that often makes programs even less effective and responsive.

Unleashing the auditors

Good information is the mother's milk of good management. The history of troubled programs, however, illustrates just how poor information about program performance can be. Defense Department managers committed themselves to buying the Divad on the basis of Army-prepared studies that exaggerated the gun's effectiveness. Federal student loan program administrators managed a program in which many key decisions were made by state officials and private bankers. FAA officials learned only after the DC-8 crash in Gander about many of the plane's mishaps. As we have seen, the lack of good information is a recurring obstacle to effective performance. One shuttle astronaut, Joseph Allen, said, "There was not a single member of that astronaut office who did not feel a profound sense of betrayal at not being told about the O-rings." [34]

When information problems occur, government often dispatches more information collectors. When problems with spare parts procurement surfaced, in fact, the first Pentagon response was to unleash an army of auditors. While accounting unquestionably has an important role to play in improving government information, and thus management, it has shortcomings. Increasing the number of auditors can weaken, rather than strengthen, administration. The Packard Commission concluded that "a plethora of departmental auditors and other overseers—and the burgeoning directives pertaining to procurement— also have tended to establish a dysfunctional relationship between DoD and its contractors." [35] No conceivable number of auditors, in the end, can fully guarantee either accountability or performance.

Furthermore, as a profession, accounting focuses on the short term, on transactions, and especially on cash transactions. A large part of government by proxy, especially regulation, guaranteed loan programs, and tax expenditures, however, does not involve cash transactions. The accounting profession has been hard pressed to move beyond the search for precision and certainty to deal with the complex issues of government by proxy. [36]

Looking to the accountants and auditors to solve program management problems often simply aggravates the regulation-recentralization reflex. Too many watchers can get in the way of performance, and too many rules and standards can hinder a private-sector organization's function. Better auditing, accounting, and program evaluation can improve management information. But the evaluation must be managed carefully to avoid creating even more problems and interfering with the program being measured.

Twin pathologies

Government by proxy thus adds formidable problems to the task of policy implementation. It undercuts the prevailing allegiance to hierarchy and control in public administration and tempts politicians and managers to respond to problems by writing rules, recentralizing program administration, or unleashing auditors. Sometimes these strategies work. More often, however, they add a new layer of their own problems to the already difficult task of managing programs indirectly.

These temptations, in fact, create a dual pathology. Managerial strategies tend to be shaped by atypical events—especially crises—in which managers have little information. That in turn gives disproportionate influence to interest groups and other parts of the issue network that are well equipped to seize the agenda with headline-grabbing horror stories. Sometimes, of course, the crises are genuine and the horror stories reflect real abuses that must be stopped. In general, though, the danger is that overall program performance and the public interest may be sacrificed to a more narrow agenda because of the ability of these interest groups to define the issues and capture public attention. Neither of these pathologies is unique to government by proxy. But both unquestionably are exacerbated by the indirect chain that exists between government-as-service-provider and the proxies who produce the services.

The implementation of government programs therefore is often not just a matter of achieving and exercising control, for this approach presumes arrangements of hierarchy and authority that do not really exist. In government by proxy, control is thus inevitably doomed to fail. As Harlan Cleveland pointed out, we are living in "the twilight of hierarchy." [37]

Managing for success

The litany of program abuses depicted in the media, reinforced by the case studies in earlier chapters of this book, may make failure seem inevitable. That, however, is not the message of this book. We have seen triumphs to match the failures and have seen as well that careful management geared to the special needs of each government-by-proxy strategy can lead to success.

The keystone of government by proxy is increasing *interdependence* between government and its proxies. The boundaries between federal, state, and local governments are more and more blurred, and the distinction between the public and private sectors is losing its meaning as government relies more on private persons and organizations for government services. This means, in turn, that government by proxy is different from other forms of management based on authority. Proxies cannot simply be ordered about. Furthermore, government-by-proxy strategies, being different from one another, require subtle, sophisticated techniques tailored to the special features of each strategy. Managing this public-private interdependence means finding a way of aligning goals and of collecting feedback.

Aligning goals

Matching goals is always difficult in a program involving different organizations. The goals of proxies rarely match the government's objectives precisely. As the cases illustrate, government by proxy adds a further twist to this problem because the government has considerable difficulty deciding just what its program goals are. Acts of Congress are notoriously vague and need to be interpreted through administrative regulations. Such regulations, in addition, are often subjected to court challenge and thus further reinterpretation. As programs evolve, moreover, they often take on subtly different casts. Thus, the government's own definition of its goals is characteristically loose, and the process of tightening that definition is a lively, dynamic one. If the goals are ill-defined, the job of meshing them with the government's proxies will be inherently difficult.

The technical complexity of many government programs also magnifies government-by-proxy problems. Even if the government knows what it wants and can get the proxy to agree to do it, the job sometimes cannot be done. Many government goods, whether new weapons or experimental drugs, ride the cutting edge of research and thus bear a certain amount of risk and uncertainty. The goals for many government services, like consultants' studies, are often deceptively hard to define. Thus, layered on top of the problems of getting agreement on goals is the further difficulty of deciding just what the goals are. Government and its proxies nevertheless share the responsibility for defining the goals—and for the final performance of many governmental programs.

Getting feedback

Finding out what happens in government programs is obviously crucial, for the flow of information is necessary to ensuring accountability. The very structure of bureaucracy often distorts the flow of information, but government by proxy worsens the problem. As hard as it is to get useful information up the chain of command within a bureaucracy, it is even more difficult to get good, reliable information from outside an organization. The incentive, in fact, often is to try to disguise problems, as practiced income-tax evaders would recognize.

The very fact that goals are ill-defined magnifies the problem. The more vague the goal, the more important good feedback becomes. Feedback from the proxy informs decision makers about the outcome of their programs and helps them fine-tune their objectives. "Policy implementation," as Martin A. Levin and Barbara Ferman point out, "is a testing and feedback process." In fact, implementation can be understood as "error correction." [38] Information helps identify defects in the program and their causes and, thus, is the mother's milk of good management.

The search for reliable information, however, collides with the bias for certainty. Such a search is based on an evolutionary notion of policy implementation: the government will begin a program, probably with ill-defined goals; it will start implementing the program; problems inevitably will crop up, but good feedback and evaluation will help identify their causes; the problems will be fixed where possible; and the cycle will begin again.

Identifying problems, however, sometimes triggers the horror-story syndrome, which in turn often forces both government officials and their proxies into a defensive, bunker mentality and initiates the regulatory-recentralization reflex. Because they make lively newspaper and television stories, tales of problems create irresistible opportunities for headline grabbing by members of Congress and by interest groups. Oversimplified for a mass audience, these stories become hooks on which to hang a judgment of an entire program. Both government officials and their proxies thus often try to minimize their risks to avoid being tainted by the horror stories.

There certainly is nothing wrong with management aimed at avoiding problems. Paradoxically, however, the drive to minimize risks in the short run often leads to bigger catastrophes in the long run. Progress usually comes more rapidly by venturing forth in small steps, making mistakes, and then learning from them. Government by proxy magnifies the inherent problem of risk avoidance, since the very nature of the policy strategies increases the risks. The danger is that by being unable to allow government to make mistakes we lose the opportunity to learn from them—and to avoid bigger problems in the future.

Finding success

Failures are not an inevitable feature of government by proxy, as the case studies in this book clearly demonstrate. What created the success stories in the preceding chapters was the ability of their managers to meet the twin challenges of government by proxy: achieving the "coalignment" of goals described by administrative theorist James D. Thompson and getting feedback about performance. Program managers used the feedback to fine-tune their management and adjusted their approaches to the subtly different features of each of the strategies.

We can examine these approaches to managing government by proxy in Figure 7-1. The coalignment of goals can be developed directly, through bargaining between government and its proxy, or indirectly, through incentives contained in the program. Feedback can come by direct observation through the government's administrative system or by indirect information produced by the political system.

Figure 7-1 Resolving the problem of goals and feedback in four government-by-proxy strategies

ALIGNING GOALS

	Direct (bargaining)	Indirect (incentives)
Direct (administrative system)	Contracts	Tax Expenditures
GETTING FEEDBACK		
Indirect (political system)	Grants	Loans

Contracts.   Contracts are, at their core, negotiated documents. The contractor agrees to do what the government wants done for an agreed-upon price. This does not mean, of course, that the purpose or price is always clear; the ambiguity, however, is part of the bargaining process. Many kinds of government contracts allow fine-tuning along the way. In contracts, furthermore, the government's feedback is direct. By looking at the good or service produced, government administrators can judge what they are getting for their money. Accurately evaluating the product's quality is not always easy, but the product is at least at hand, in contrast to other strategies.

Grants.   Intergovernmental grants are a practical accommodation to the American system of federalism. The federal government agrees to grant money if state or local governments will conduct certain programs. Precisely what is to be done with the grant is often determined through negotiation among federal, state, and local officials. Finding out where the money goes, however, is usually a difficult proposition. The performance reports of grantees often contain very little useful information. Feedback through the political process—in the form of complaints, charges, and demands from citizens—often provides far better information about what actually happens to the money.

Tax expenditures.   The government has no such problem with tax expenditures. The tax returns filed by each individual and corporation provide clear evidence about how the tax preference is being used. Of course, the full range of the tax expenditure's economic effects remains unclear, but the basic information is present. Unlike contracts, however, the impact of the tax expenditure is not the result of a compromise between government and its proxy. Rather, the government creates an incentive in the tax expenditure and it is up to the proxy to decide how (and even whether) to use it. Coalignment of goals thus occurs through an indirect process.

Loans.   Like tax expenditures, government loans rely on incentives for alignment of goals. The government creates a loan program, with certain eligibility criteria and program features. Those individuals who wish to subject themselves to the program's requirements take out the loans. However, as with grants, feedback on the loans and their use is difficult to obtain. The government's accounting system makes measurement of lending programs difficult, and the final use of the money is often impossible to determine. The complaints and pressures of the wider political system, rather than the programs' own administrative features, provide the best feedback.

Regulation. Regulation is missing from Figure 7-1 because it is a hybrid strategy. Alignment of values comes through command: the government as regulator issues orders, and the proxies as regulatees must obey. (The content of the regulations is negotiated during the political process, of course. Once the rules are promulgated, though, the regulatee is bound by them.) Feedback comes through several channels, through direct government inspection, indirectly through political processes such as elections and negotiations, and through catastrophic accidents such as the *Challenger* explosion.

Proxy on proxy

We can add one further complication to the conduct of government by proxy. These proxies often do not operate alone; instead several proxies work simultaneously on one program. For example, a typical community development project can be an extremely elaborate undertaking. A federal grant might provide the money to clear a site for rehabilitation. The local government receiving the grant would then hire a private contractor to remove the buildings and prepare the site for construction. Different federal or state grant programs might provide the funds for construction. The project must be administered throughout according to not only the regulations of each program but also a complicated set of crosscutting regulations. These regulations enforce federal standards—for instance, on equal employment and environmental protection. One project can thus involve all of the proxy strategies we have explored.[39]

It is not unusual, therefore, to layer proxies upon proxies and thereby to compound the advantages as well as the political and administrative difficulties of each program. What holds all of this together is regulation, which is not only a strategy in its own right but also the means of controlling all of the other strategies.

Leadership

Since each government-by-proxy strategy poses different problems for goals and feedback, no one administrative approach is appropriate for all. This presents a basic challenge to government managers: they must be able to diagnose the special administrative and political problems of the strategy they are using and then to adapt their managerial techniques to solve these problems. This, in turn, requires increased sophistication in government managers. Managers, as analyst and former federal official Laurence E. Lynn, Jr., contends, must "take the time to manage." [40] They must ensure that they are not ensnared by the short-term bias toward certainty at the expense of solving long-term problems.

Government managers, in short, must be leaders. As Robert C. Tucker put it, their fundamental task is a "diagnostic function," to "define the situation authoritatively for the group." [41] Administrative leaders must be able to recognize that different government strategies present different managerial problems; to be aware of the particular problems that a given strategy presents; and to develop an approach to solving them.

Of all the government-by-proxy strategies, contracts and loans are spreading most rapidly. Contracts theoretically offer the promise of more productivity for the same amount of money as that spent on direct programs; loans offer the promise (but sometimes not the reality) of programs that spend relatively little money. The two strategies pose very different problems for administrative leaders. For contracts to work, according to theory, the bargain (and, in particular, the objective) must be clear in advance. Rarely, however, can government decide in advance exactly what it wants or needs. Military weapons, for instance, are technological innovations, and their objectives are evolving. Political pressures often alter goals in other contracts. In such circumstances, therefore, administrative leaders must demonstrate great skill not only in negotiating the original contract but in bargaining their way through the inevitable changes that occur after the program begins.

Loan programs require a different kind of leadership skill, a skill in anticipating the incentives—and disincentives—a program might create and in managing the program accordingly. Will eligibility changes make a loan program relatively more attractive to "risky" applicants and thus make defaults more likely? Will shifting economic conditions undermine the stability of the program? These leadership skills call for more sophisticated managers and more advanced training to prepare them for the challenges they face.

Accountability and performance _____

Through a fascinating variety of rationales—from traditional American concerns for self-government to more modern public choice theory, from a planned response to technological challenges to pragmatic reactions to tighter budgets—U.S. government since World War II has become ever more reliant on proxies for the performance of its functions. It is a tangled web, indeed. We have greater expectations about what government ought to do and greater skepticism about government's ability to do it. The result has been more sharing of responsibility for government programs with the private sector, both corporations and individuals, to the point of blurring the dividing line between "public" and "private." Government officials, meanwhile, have responsibility "for programs they do not really control." [42]

This book provides two responses to the prevailing suspicion that government programs do not work well. First, the roots of many of the problems lie in the deep complexity of the policy strategies themselves. Government by proxy poses great challenges to both government and its proxies to work interdependently. Second, the route to success is through recognizing the nature of government by proxy and the varying managerial problems posed by different strategies, and then developing imaginative approaches to solving these problems.

Democratic accountability is an even more serious concern in managing government by proxy. The sharing of authority between government and its proxies, as Salamon pointed out, is a central feature of these strategies. At the same time, each program has a public interest, however vaguely defined, that transcends a program's collection of private interests. The challenge to the nation's political institutions is to promote the reconciliation of the different values of government and its proxies, without sacrificing the public interest at the core of each program. This poses a great political and administrative challenge.

As government by proxy has grown, the success of government programs has come to depend more on all Americans and their sense of citizenship. All of those responsible for the performance of government—whether part of government or not—must recognize their broader responsibility to the public for their behavior. Accountability thus has to extend beyond creating government mechanisms to detect and cure problems. Whether filling out an income tax form, taking out a government loan, following a federal regulation, or working for a government contractor, each citizen plays an important role in making programs work. Each of our individual actions, added together, determines the results of governmental policy. Government by proxy thus emphasizes with great clarity the obligations of citizenship, for, as its strategies grow, government and its performance depend increasingly on all of us.

161

Notes

1. U.S. Presidential Commission on the Space Shuttle Challenger Accident (Rogers Commission), *Report to the President* (Washington, D.C.: U.S. Government Printing Office, 1986).
2. Ibid., 120.
3. Ibid., 64, 71.
4. Ibid., 90.
5. Ibid., 93.
6. Ibid., 94, 96.
7. Ibid., 84.
8. Anthony Downs, *Inside Bureaucracy* (Boston: Little, Brown, 1967), 77, 116-118.
9. Charles Peters, "From Ouagadougou to Cape Canaveral: Why the Bad News Doesn't Travel Up," *Washington Monthly*, April 1986, 27.
10. Rogers Commission, *Report*, 104.
11. *Wall Street Journal*, June 11, 1986, 3.
12. U.S. Congress, House of Representatives, Committee on Science and Technology, *Investigation of the Challenger Accident*, report, 99th Cong., 2d sess., 1986, 6.
13. *Washington Post*, May 8, 1986, A1.
14. *New York Times*, April 23, 1986, A14-15.
15. House Science and Technology Committee, *Investigation of the Challenger Accident*, 172, 173.
16. The House Committee, however, feels that the problem was not NASA's management structure but "poor technical decision making." The report suggests that managers did not interpret adequately the messages they were getting about the O-rings, a form of distortion that does not really contradict the Rogers Commission's findings. Ibid., 4.
17. James D. Thompson, *Organizations in Action* (New York: McGraw-Hill, 1967), 152.
18. *New York Times*, June 29, 1986, Sec. 3, 8.
19. House Science and Technology Committee, *Investigation of the Challenger Accident*, 179.
20. Rogers Commission, *Report*, 104.
21. Ibid., 164.
22. *New York Times*, June 29, 1986, Sec. 3, 8. House Science and Technology Committee, *Investigation of the Challenger Accident*, 3.
23. *New York Times*, June 29, 1986, Sec. 3, 1.
24. Randall B. Ripley and Grace A. Franklin, *Policy Implementation and Bureaucracy*, 2d ed. (Chicago: Dorsey Press, 1986), 2.
25. Eugene Bardach, *The Implementation Game* (Cambridge: MIT Press, 1977), 283.
26. Jeffrey L. Pressman and Aaron Wildavsky, *Implementation*, 3d ed. (Berkeley: University of California Press, 1984); and Brian W. Hogwood and B. Guy Peters, *The Pathology of Public Policy* (New York: Oxford University Press, 1985).
27. Richard E. Neustadt, *Presidential Power* (New York: John Wiley, 1960), 9.
28. R. James Woolsey, speech to National Academy of Public Administration, Spring Meeting, Washington, D.C., June 5, 1986.
29. President's Blue Ribbon Commission on Defense Management (Packard

Commission), *Report to the President* (Washington, D.C.: U.S. Government Printing Office, 1986).
30. Donald F. Kettl, *The Regulation of American Federalism* (Baton Rouge: Louisiana State University Press, 1983).
31. Rogers Commission, *Report*, 199.
32. Brian O'Connell, speech to National Academy of Public Administration, Spring Meeting, Washington, D.C., June 5, 1986.
33. James W. Fesler, "Approaches to the Understanding of Decentralization," *Journal of Politics* 27 (August 1965): 536-566.
34. James Reston, Jr., "The Astronauts After Challenger," *New York Times Magazine*, January 25, 1987, 52.
35. Packard Commission, *Report to the President*, 75-76.
36. Herman B. Leonard, *Checks Unbalanced* (New York: Basic Books, 1986), 207-221.
37. Harlan Cleveland, "Control: The Twilight of Hierarchy," *New Management* 3 (Fall 1985): 14-25.
38. Martin A. Levin and Barbara Ferman, *The Political Hand* (New York: Pergamon Press, 1985), 14.
39. See Kettl, *The Regulation of American Federalism.*
40. Laurence E. Lynn, Jr., *Managing the Public's Business* (New York: Basic Books, 1981), 181. Compare Steve Kelman, "The Grace Commission: How Much Waste in Government?" *The Public Interest*, no. 78 (Winter 1985): 80.
41. Robert C. Tucker, *Politics as Leadership* (Columbia: University of Missouri Press, 1981), 18-19.
42. Lester M. Salamon, "Rethinking Public Management: Third-Party Government and the Changing Forms of Government Action," *Public Policy* 29 (Summer 1981): 260.

Index ══